CAMBRIDGE LIBRARY COLLECTION

Books of enduring scholarly value

Travel and Exploration

The history of travel writing dates back to the Bible, Caesar, the Vikings and the Crusaders, and its many themes include war, trade, science and recreation. Explorers from Columbus to Cook charted lands not previously visited by Western travellers, and were followed by merchants, missionaries, and colonists, who wrote accounts of their experiences. The development of steam power in the nineteenth century provided opportunities for increasing numbers of 'ordinary' people to travel further, more economically, and more safely, and resulted in great enthusiasm for travel writing among the reading public. Works included in this series range from first-hand descriptions of previously unrecorded places, to literary accounts of the strange habits of foreigners, to examples of the burgeoning numbers of guidebooks produced to satisfy the needs of a new kind of traveller - the tourist.

Through South Africa

Henry Morton Stanley (1841–1904), the Welsh-born explorer famous for his 1871 meeting with the missionary David Livingstone, travelled widely in Africa. First published in 1898, this is a compendium of letters written by Stanley during his travels to Bulawayo, Johannesburg and Pretoria, which lend a unique insight into colonial South Africa in the late nineteenth century. Focusing on the country's culture and commercial development, he recalls his impressions of industries such as railways, farms and gold mines, social issues such as immigration and poverty, and the contentious relations between the Boer peoples and the British colonists which led to the Second Boer War. Through his passionate exposition, we learn of his adversity towards President Kruger's policies, and his compassion for the people who he claims were left to starve because the government's priorities were military. His memoirs provide a revealing snapshot of an important period in South Africa's history.

T0381633

Cambridge University Press has long been a pioneer in the reissuing of out-of-print titles from its own backlist, producing digital reprints of books that are still sought after by scholars and students but could not be reprinted economically using traditional technology. The Cambridge Library Collection extends this activity to a wider range of books which are still of importance to researchers and professionals, either for the source material they contain, or as landmarks in the history of their academic discipline.

Drawing from the world-renowned collections in the Cambridge University Library, and guided by the advice of experts in each subject area, Cambridge University Press is using state-of-the-art scanning machines in its own Printing House to capture the content of each book selected for inclusion. The files are processed to give a consistently clear, crisp image, and the books finished to the high quality standard for which the Press is recognised around the world. The latest print-on-demand technology ensures that the books will remain available indefinitely, and that orders for single or multiple copies can quickly be supplied.

The Cambridge Library Collection will bring back to life books of enduring scholarly value (including out-of-copyright works originally issued by other publishers) across a wide range of disciplines in the humanities and social sciences and in science and technology.

Through South Africa

H ENRY M ORTON S TANLEY

CAMBRIDGE UNIVERSITY PRESS

Cambridge, New York, Melbourne, Madrid, Cape Town,
Singapore, São Paolo, Delhi, Tokyo, Mexico City

Published in the United States of America by Cambridge University Press, New York

www.cambridge.org
Information on this title: www.cambridge.org/9781108031172

This edition first published 1898
This digitally printed version 2011

ISBN 978-1-108-03117-2 Paperback

THROUGH SOUTH AFRICA

HIS HONOUR PRESIDENT KRUGER. *[Frontispiece.*

THROUGH
SOUTH AFRICA

BY

HENRY M. STANLEY, M.P., D.C.L.

AUTHOR OF
"HOW I FOUND LIVINGSTONE," "IN DARKEST AFRICA"
"THROUGH THE DARK CONTINENT," ETC.

BEING

AN ACCOUNT OF HIS RECENT VISIT TO RHODESIA
THE TRANSVAAL, CAPE COLONY, AND NATAL

REPRINTED, WITH ADDITIONS, FROM "SOUTH AFRICA'

With Map and several Illustrations

LONDON
SAMPSON LOW, MARSTON AND COMPANY
LIMITED
St. Dunstan's House
FETTER LANE, FLEET STREET, E.C.
1898

 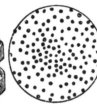

PREFACE.

THIS little volume consists of the letters I wrote
from Bulawayo, Johannesburg and Pretoria for
the journal *South Africa*, which is exclusively
devoted to matters relating to the region whence
it derives its title. Each letter contains the
researches of a week. As the public had already
a sufficiency of books dealing with the history,
geography, politics, raids and revolts, I confined
myself to such impressions as one, who since
1867 had been closely connected with equatorial,
northern and western Africa, might derive from a
first view of the interior of South Africa. Being
in no way associated with any political or pecuniary
concern relating to the country, it struck me that
my open-minded, disinterested and fresh impressions might be of some interest to others, who like
myself had only a general sympathy with its
civilisation and commercial development. And as
I had necessarily to qualify myself for appearing
in a journal which had for years treated of South
African subjects, it involved much personal inquiry

and careful consideration of facts communicated to
me, and an impartial weighing of their merits. To
this motive, whatever may be the value of what I
have written, I am greatly indebted personally ; for
henceforth I must carry with me for a long time a
valuable kind of knowledge concerning the colonies
and states I traversed, which no number of books
could have given to me.

If, from my point of judgment, I differ in any
way from other writers, all I care to urge is,
that I have had some experience of my own in
several new lands like the South African interior,
and I have lived long enough to have seen the
effects of what was good and what was bad
policy in them. I prefer peaceful relations
between England and the Boers of South Africa,
if possible ; I love what is just, fair, and best to
and for both Britons and Boers. I naturally
admire large-minded enterprise. I pity narrow-
mindedness, and dislike to see a people refusing
to advance, when all the world is so sympathetic
and helpfully inclined towards them. These
explanations, I think, will enable anyone to understand the spirit of these letters.

A curious thing occurred in connection with
my sudden departure for South Africa. In the
latter part of September, 1897, I was debating
with my family, at a seaside hotel near Dieppe,
as to the place we should visit after the adjourn-
ment of Parliament in 1898. After discussing

the merits of many suggestions, it was finally determined that we should all try South Africa, because it was said to have such a divine climate ; the country was, moreover, so interesting politically, and as it loomed so much in public interest it would be worth while to obtain some personal knowledge of South Africans at home. We had scarcely arrived at this conclusion, when the postman brought to us a telegram, which, to our intense surprise, was a request from the Bulawayo Festivities Committee that I would go to Bula-wayo to attend the celebration of the arrival of the Great Peninsular Railway at the Capital of Matabele Land. We regarded it as a strange coincidence.

This opportunity to visit Bulawayo I considered rather premature, as towards the end of autumn many engagements crowd upon one, but after another animated family council it was resolved that I should accept the invitation were it only to qualify myself as a pioneer for the ladies.

We left Southampton on the *Norman* on the 9th October. I found then that there were five other members of the House of Commons on board —Messrs. Saunderson, Llewellyn, Hayes Fisher, Peace, and Paullton, and the Duke of Roxburghe representing the House of Lords. Among the passengers there were Boers from Pretoria and Cape Colony, British Uitlanders from Johannesburg, English residents from the Cape and the two

Dutch Republics, Afrikander farmers and vine-growers, and townspeople, some from the Cape District, others from the Eastern and Western Provinces, and not a few from Kimberley and Natal, besides a few ex-Raiders and Reformers. As may be imagined, there was no lack of instructive material, and naturally much divergence of political opinion. The smoking-room soon become like a debating club, but, notwithstanding the frankness and partisan character of the debates, the good temper with which each person delivered himself of his opinions was most astonishing.

From the Boers and Afrikanders I heard not one favourable remark about England, but all indulged in banter and irony, to prove that argument with them was of no avail. So extreme was their dislike that they even said "English servants and clerks are of no use, and they are most unreliable, as for instance," and here followed incidents to prove what they said. While the English were false and could not be trusted, it was said that the Germans were "good" in the colonial sense, and made the best citizens. They were industrious and thrifty, and their improved condition did not alter their habits. The in-denturing of the Bechuana rebels was a subject upon which much was said on both sides. But a Boer's way of putting it was characteristic. "England, you say, considers it illegal. Ah, well, the English know nothing of the matter, and what they say don't count. Rose-Innes, however, ought to have known better. Had he been asked by a Cape farmer whether, to keep the rebels from starving, we should give them work to do for wages, Rose-Innes would have said, ' It is a good thing, and the best that can be done for them ' ; but with the view of forming a party against the Government, of course, he denounces indenturing as illegal and iniquitous." I have cited these extracts to show the process of how we became initiated into South African politics.

The treatment of natives by the Rhodesian Government was, according to the general opinion of Cape people, more liberal than they deserved, and such as any white colonist of no matter what country would approve. It was said, " Why, if we were to be governed by what these senti- mental English societies—referring to the A.P.S. —think is right, we should have to abandon Africa altogether, for neither our lives nor property would be safe. Law-abiding men and lawless natives cannot live together unless one or the other is compelled to, and as we have taken the country and intend to live in it, common sense tells us that the natives must submit to the same law under which we must live."

The greatest majority by far denounced the Raid, and yet everyone spoke kindly of the personality of Dr. Jameson. A gentleman from the Eastern Province informed me that the Jameson family has suffered greatly in public estimation. One of the brothers who lived at King Williamstown had felt himself obliged to leave the Province and return to England, and if the Doctor succeeded in being elected to the Cape Parliament, it was said he would be certain to meet with much unpleasantness.

I believe there were 1,097 souls on board the *Norman* on this voyage. The noise was therefore terrific and continuous, and if any of the weaker constitutions suffered as much as I did through want of sleep and rest, they must on arrival at Cape Town have been in a pitiable state. Above and below it was perpetual unrest and uproar. Though large and beautiful, these Cape steamers are badly designed internally, and the cabins are extremely small, and so arranged that a passenger is subject to the caprices of his neighbours on either side. My neighbours were unfortunately quite ignorant of the meaning of the word "considerate." When an Ismay, such as he who reformed the Anglo-American service, becomes interested in the passenger traffic to the Cape, he will find a multitude of little things to improve. On returning to England, I found the s.s. *Moor* much superior for passenger accommodation.

The inconveniences arising from an overcrowded steamer are too many to be disposed of in a

paragraph, but it is enough to say that I was
uncommonly glad when the voyage was ended, and
I was free to seek a hotel.

It must impress anyone who takes a sympathetic
interest in what he sees in South Africa, that in
some things the country is far behind New Zealand,
Tasmania, or any of the Australian Colonies.
It is more backward than any of them in its
hotels. There are, within my knowledge, only
three hotels in all South Africa to which I would
venture to recommend a lady to go. South
Africans, of course, are able to endure anything,
and as the Veld is comparatively but a step
from most towns, any place that offers a decent
lodging must be regarded by the men at least as
infinitely superior to an ox-wagon, a zinc hut, or a
farm shed. But I am thinking more of the effect
such hotels as those of Cape Town must have on
people from Europe. This city, which is the
capital of Cape Colony, contains a population of
about 52,000, exclusive of the suburbs, but it does
not possess a single hotel that would bear comparison with those of Sydney, Melbourne, Adelaide,
Auckland, Christchurch or Dunedin. The very
best is only just suited for commercial travellers,
who must needs be satisfied with whatever may
offer. The suburbs, however, which are peopled by
about 32,000—and it is well that invalids and
tourists should remember it—contain hotels where
rest and quiet may be found, in the midst of oak

and fir groves and scenes of surpassing beauty.
No city that I know of in our colonies possesses
superior suburbs. They are simply lovely. They
are stretched along the base of Table Mountain,
and an entire day's carriage-drive would not
exhaust the exquisite beauty for which the
suburbs of Cape Town are famed.

Cape Colony possesses three valuable assets,
which seem to me to have received scant attention.
A traveller who has visited Southern California
and Arizona will understand immediately he visits
South Africa what fortunes might be made of the
waste land, the rainfall, and the glorious climate
with which Nature has blessed it. The land is
unworthily despised, the rainfall is allowed to
waste itself in thirsty sands deep down beneath
the level of hungry plains, while the climate does
not seem to have suggested to any capitalist
that a revenue superior to that obtained from the
Main Reef at Johannesburg might be drawn
from it. The leaders of South African enterprise
appear all absorbed in diamonds, gold mines, or
dynamite.

If I were to follow the authorities of Worsfold in
his "South Africa," pp. 126, 127, I should have to
admit that this indifference to the land, the rainfall
and climate, is due to the Boers. Captain Percival,
in 1796, a hundred years ago, wrote :—

"The Dutch farmers never assist the soil by
flooding ; their only labour is sowing the seed,

leaving the rest to chance and the excellent climate."

"No part of the world has had its natura advantages so abused as the Cape of Good Hope. The very minds and dispositions of the settlers interfere with every plan of improvement and public utility."

It may be that the Boers do cling to old-fashioned ideas somewhat more tenaciously than they ought to do; but they cannot possibly interfere with capitalists uniting to build up-to-date hotels on the most salubrious and scenic sites in Cape Colony, and beautifying their neighbour-hoods with shade trees and gardens, so that the thousands of invalids who throng the watering-places and hydros of Europe, endure the snows of Davos, and the winter of the Engadine, might be tempted to try the Karroo of the Colony. They did not interfere with John D. Logan when he bought 100,000 acres of the Karroo at Matjesfontein and proceeded to turn it to remunerative account. They do not object to private companies or in-dividuals making irrigation works, or planting groves, which thrive so wonderfully; and as Cape Colony has been British for over ninety years, it is rather hard that the Boers should bear all the blame.

Now the Cape Government may well plead guilty to having left many things undone which they ought to have done. I sincerely believe that the time will come when the climate, which has the quality of making old men young, and the consumptive strong, will become universally known and appreciated; but to attract invalids from the crowded Riviera and Switzerland, visitors must not be lodged in third-rate hotels, near noisy tram-lines, and fed on tinned meats.

I was about concluding this preface, when a South African appeared at my house and drew my attention to the Scriptural quotation in my Johannesburg letter—"It is expedient that one man should die for many," and begged me to make my meaning clear. I read the paragraph over again, and as I see that to a wilfully contentious mind it might be construed into a meaning very different to what I intended, I will try to make it clearer.

Certain Johannesburgers at the Club had related to us the story of the various efforts they had made to obtain their political rights, and the reforms which were needed to work their mines profitably; and after they had finished, I replied that everyone was well aware of the demonstrations, mass-meetings, speeches, petitions to Kruger, menaces, Jameson's Raid, and so on, and they themselves had just informed me how often they had yielded to bribery of officials, and yet withal they confessed they were not a whit further advanced. Their position had not been bettered, but was somewhat worse. "The corrective of it all," I said, "seems to me to lie in the Scriptural

verse, 'It is expedient that one man should
die for many.' There is a vast mass of sympathy in England with you, but it is inert and
inactive. To make that sympathy a living force in
your behalf, it must be proved that you are in
earnest, that nothing sordid lies behind this dis-
satisfaction. You must prove that you have a
cause for which you are willing to suffer, even to
the death. You say that you can do nothing without arms. You do not need any arms that I see.
If you fight with weapons, you will be overcome,
and I do not think your defeat will excite great
sympathy. But if it be true that the impositions
on you are intolerable, your taxes heavy, the
claims of Government extortionate, and the demands excessive, why submit to them? It seems
to me that if you were all united in the determination
to pay no more of these claims, taxes and bribes,
and folded your arms and dared them to do their
worst, that Kruger must either yield or proceed to
compulsion of some kind. He would probably
confiscate your property, or put you in prison or
banish you. Whatever he does that is violent and
tyrannical will cause such an explosion of opinion
that will prove to you all that England does not
forget her children. No cause was ever won without suffering, and I am afraid that your cause,
however good it may be, cannot be won without
sacrifice and suffering of some kind. The leader of
any movement is sure to be the object of a tyrant's

hate, and the leader or leaders of your cause ought
not to venture in it without being prepared to
suffer and endure whatever ills may follow."

Having explained the Scriptural quotation at
the request of others, I now proceed to be more
definite in my own behalf with regard to the
statement in the same letter, that "we cannot
interfere until we know what Johannesburg has
resolved upon doing."

A gentleman present said that, during his recent
visit to London, an English statesman asked him,
"What would be the effect of sending 30,000
British troops to the Transvaal." Whereupon
he answered that he would be the first man who
would take up his rifle against them.

This gentleman was an Englishman by birth.
He had been the loudest and the most eloquent
against the British Government for their disregard
of the rights guaranteed by the Convention of
1884, he knew as well as anyone present the
tenour of the despatches that had been exchanged
between the British Government and the Transvaal Republic, and was perfectly acquainted with
the patient and continuous efforts the Colonial
Office had made to obtain a just consideration
for the grievances of the Uitlanders. It was
obvious to us that, if a British statesman had
asked such a question, it must have been with
the view of knowing—if diplomacy failed—what
result would follow the final attempt to induce

Kruger to listen to reason. From the shock this declaration from such a prominent Uitlander gave me and a colleague of mine, we understood what the feelings of the statesman referred to must have been, and we had no option left than to suppose the Uitlanders, despite all their clamour and affected indignation against the Transvaal Government, would prefer the Colonial Office to continue writing despatches than to take coercive measures. It must be an immense relief to Englishmen all over the country, as well as it was to me, to know that we were not expected to be at the trouble and cost of sending troops, and we may all feel sure that as despatch-writing is considered to be so efficacious, the Colonial Office will not begrudge the labour nor spare expense in stationery.

At any rate, seeing that the Uitlanders have told us frankly what to expect if we resort to force for their assistance, it is too obvious that nothing more can be done by our Government further than courteous diplomacy permits—until the united voice and the united action of the whole body of the Uitlanders certify to us in what other way England can serve them.

HENRY M. STANLEY.

LONDON, *January* 28*th*, 1898.

b

CONTENTS.

CHAPTER IV.

CHAPTER V.

CHAPTER VI.

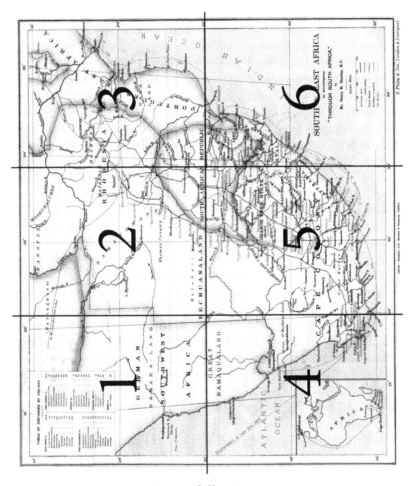

Key to following pages.

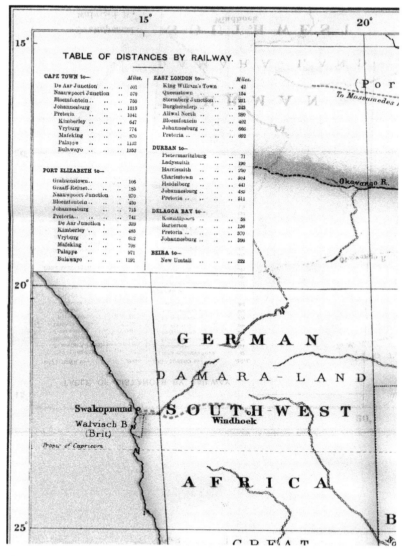

TABLE OF DISTANCES BY RAILWAY.

CAPE TOWN to—	Miles.	EAST LONDON to—	Miles.
De Aar Junction	501	King William's Town	42
Naauwpoort Junction	579	Queenstown	154
Bloemfontein	750	Stormberg Junction	221
Johannesburg	1015	Burghersdorp	243
Pretoria	1041	Aliwal North	280
Kimberley	647	Bloemfontein	402
Vryburg	774	Johannesburg	666
Mafeking	870	Pretoria	692
Palapye	1153		
Bulawayo	1353	**DURBAN to—**	
		Pietermaritzburg	71
		Ladysmith	190
PORT ELIZABETH to—		Harrismith	250
		Charlestown	304
Grahamstown	106	Heidelberg	441
Graaff-Reinet	185	Johannesburg	483
Naauwpoort Junction	270	Pretoria	511
Bloemfontein	450		
Johannesburg	715	**DELAGOA BAY to—**	
Pretoria	741	Komatipoort	58
De Aar Junction	339	Barberton	136
Kimberley	485	Pretoria	370
Vryburg	612	Johannesburg	396
Mafeking	708		
Palapye	971	**BEIRA to—**	
Bulawayo	1191	New Umtali	222

15°   20°

15°

(Por

To Mossamedes

Okavango R.

20°

GERMAN

DAMARA-LAND

Swakopmund   SOUTH-WEST

Walvisch B   Windhoek

(Brit)

Tropic of Capricorn

AFRICA

25°

GREAT

1

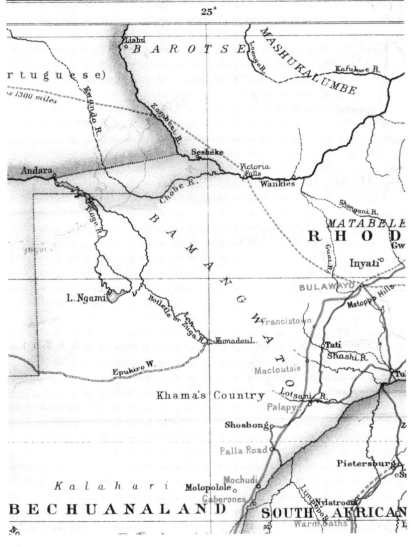

BAROTSE

MASHUKALUMBE

Liahu

Loenge R.

Kafukwe R.

(rtuguese)

1300 miles

Kwando R.

Zambesi R.

Seaheke

Victoria
Falls

Andara

Chobe R.

Wankies

Shangani R.

MATABELE

RHOD

B A M A N G W A T O

Gw

Inyati

Guai R.

BULAWAYO

Matoppo Hills

L. Ngami

Botlede or Zuga R.

Francistown

Tati

Kunadaul.

Shashi R.

Tu

Epukiro W.

Macloutsie

Khama's Country

Lotsani R.

Palapye

Shoshong

Pietersburg

Palla Road

Mochudi

K a l a h a r i

Molopolole

Gaberones

Limpopo R.

Nylstroom

BECHUANALAND

SOUTH AFRICAN

Warm Baths

2

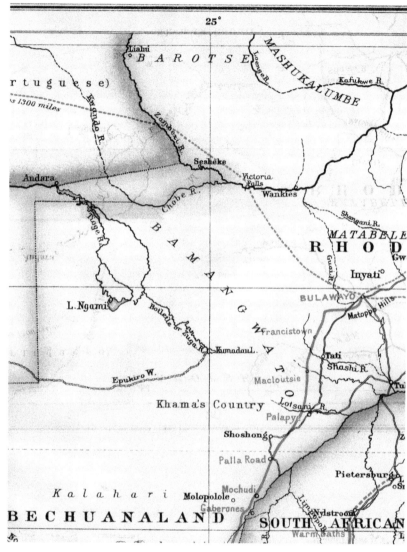

2

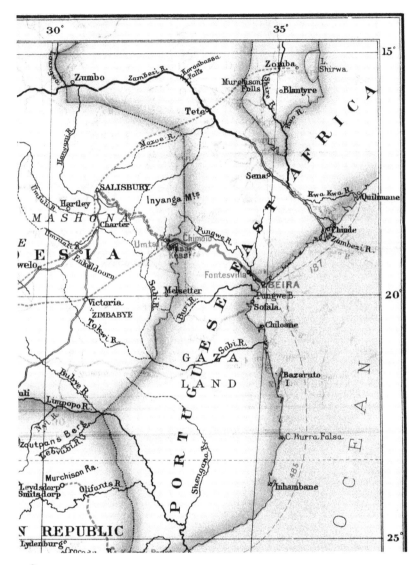

3

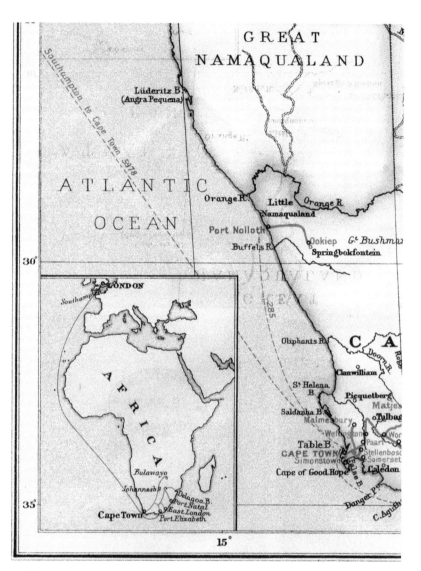

GREAT
NAMAQUALAND

Lüderitz B.
(Angra Pequena)

ATLANTIC

OCEAN

Southampton to Cape Town 5978

Orange R.

Little
Namaqualand

Orange R.

Port Nolloth

Ookiep   G.t Bushma
Springbokfontein

Buffels R.

30°

Oliphants R.

C   A

Doorn R.

Clanwilliam

St Helena
B.

Picquetberg

Matjes

Saldanha B.

Malmesbury   Tulba

Wellington   Wor

Table B.

Paarl

CAPE TOWN

Stellenbosc

Simonstown

Somerset

Cape of Good Hope

Caledon

Danger P.

C. Agulh

LONDON

Southampton

AFRICA

Bulawayo

Johannesb.

Delagoa B.

Port Natal

Cape Town

East London

Port Elizabeth

35°

15°

4

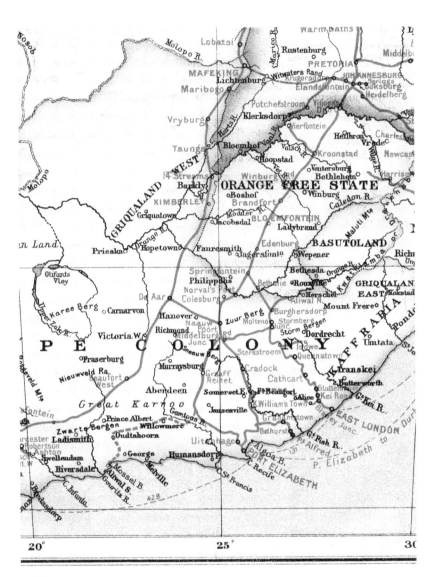

20°   25°   30

London : Sampson, Low, Marston & Company, Limited.

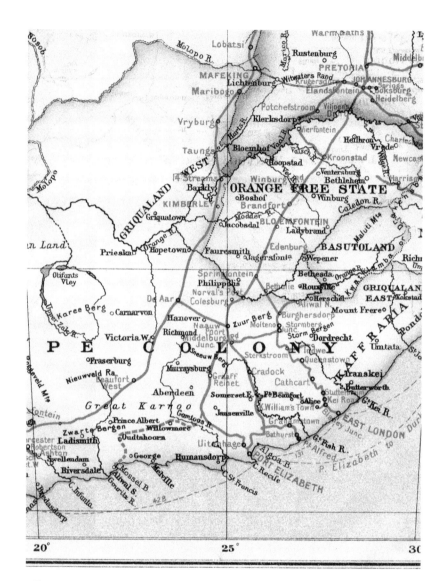

London : Sampson, Low, Marston & Company, Limited.

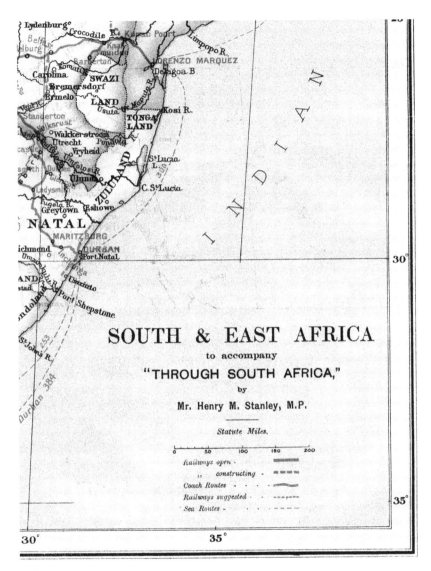

SOUTH & EAST AFRICA

to accompany

"THROUGH SOUTH AFRICA,"

by

Mr. Henry M. Stanley, M.P.

Statute Miles.

0	50	100	150	200

Railways open -
  ,,   constructing -
Coach Routes - - -
Railways suggested - - -
Sea Routes -

6

LIST OF ILLUSTRATIONS.

THROUGH
SOUTH AFRICA

CHAPTER I.

BULAWAYO, *November* 5, 1897.

THIS extraordinary town does not disappoint expectations by its progress or present condition. It is in about as advanced a state as it could well be, considering the troubles it has endured. War and cattle-plague have retarded the progressive growth of a town that would have been by this, judging from the spirit of the people, a phenomenon in a century which has seen cities grow like mushrooms. It is cast on broad lines; its streets rival those of Washington for breadth, and its houses occupy as much space as decency requires, for unless they were pulled down and scattered over their respective lots, it is scarcely possible, with due respect to height, that they could occupy more.

B

BULAWAYO.

Its situation, however, does not approach what I had anticipated to find. From its association with Lo Bengula, the dread Matabele despot on whose single word hung life and death, I had expected to find Bulawayo situate on a commanding eminence, looking down on broad lowlands and far-reaching views that fed the despot's pride of power ; instead of which we found it squatted low on a reddish plain, the ridges of its houses scarcely higher than the thorn bush that surrounds it. There are no hills or eminences anywhere in view, whence a large prospect could be obtained. In fact, the greater part of South Africa appears different to what I had imagined. Probably the partiality of all South African writers for Dutch terms had contributed to give me erroneous impressions. When I read Fenimore Cooper and Mayne Reid's descriptions of the West, I fancied I knew what a prairie or plain was, and when, years afterwards, I came in view of them my impressions were only confirmed. But high, low, and bush *veld*, and *Karroo*, etc., have been always indefinite terms to me, and so I came to conceive aspects of land which were different to the reality. For a thousand miles we have been travelling over very level or slightly undulating plains, bush-covered over large spaces, the rest being genuine grassy prairie. After a thousand miles, or nearly three days by rail, over a flat country of this description, one naturally thinks that the objective point of such a journey must be of a different character. Most of the guests were on the *qui vive* for a pleasing change of scenery until we were within five minutes of Bulawayo station. All at once we caught sight of a few gleams of zinc roofs through the low thorn bush, and a single iron smoke-stack. When we came out of the bush, Bulawayo was spread out before us, squatted on what is undeniably a plain. This plain continues to be of the same character of levelness as far as Salisbury, ay, even as far as the northern edge of Mashonaland ; it spreads out to Fort Victoria equally level ; and as the land declines to N'gami and the Victoria Falls, it still retains the appearance of plains. Now, the wonder to me is, not that I am 1360 miles north of Cape Town, but that the railway limit should be fixed at Bulawayo, a mere bit of undistinguishable acreage in a flat area which extends to over half a million square miles. Why this place more than any other ? There is no river near it, there is no topographic feature to distinguish it. Why not have continued this trunk line on to Salisbury, on to Tete, and the Zambesi ? Why not have continued it on to the Victoria Falls ?

THE NEW RAILWAY.

Considering that we have come all the way from London, 7300 miles away, to celebrate the arrival of the locomotive at Bulawayo, such questions may sound ungrateful, and considering that last night at the banquet every speaker had something favourable to say of the Bechuanaland Railway and its builders, such questions may be supposed to indicate disagreement with the general opinion. There is really no necessity to suppose anything of the kind. Both the builders and the railway deserve praise. The fact that some eight trains have already arrived at Bulawayo, and that every passenger expresses himself warmly as to the condition of the line, and the pleasure derived from the journey, ought to satisfy everyone that the railway is ready for traffic, and will serve for many years, I hope, to connect Bulawayo with Cape Town.

But I want my readers to thoroughly understand what has been done, without prejudice to Bulawayo, the railway, or its builders. I am not so surprised at the railway, as at the length of time people in South Africa were content to be without it. The whole country seems to have been created for railway making. It offers as few difficulties as the London Embankment. Hyde Park is extremely uneven as compared with it.

For nearly a thousand miles the railway sleepers have been laid at intervals of thirty inches on the natural face of the land ; the rails have been laid across these, and connected together ; the native navvies have scraped a little soil together, sufficient to cover the steel sleepers ; and the iron road was thus ready for traffic. In March, 1896, the railway was but a few miles beyond Mafeking—say, about 880 miles from Cape Town—on November 4, 1897, it is 1360 miles in length from Cape Town, showing a construction of 480 miles in 19 months. There is nothing remarkable in this. The Union Pacific Railway between Omaha and Denver progressed at three, four, even five miles a day, over a much more irregular surface ; but then, of course, the navvies were Irishmen, who handled the shovel like experts, and the rails with the precision and skill of master workmen. Natives could not be expected to attain the proficiency and organisation of the American Celts.

In One of the Cape Specials.

Our special train left Cape Town on Sunday at 4 P.M. A corridor train of six coaches, marked Bulawayo, at an ordinary provincial - looking station, seemed somewhat strange. Had it been marked Ujiji, or Yambuya, it could not have been more so. Three of us were put in a compartment for four. The fourth berth was available for hand

luggage.   Soon after starting we were served with
tea and biscuits, and were it not for the flat wilder-
ness scenery we might have imagined ourselves in
an International sleeping car.   Time tables were
also furnished us, from which we learned that we
were due at Kimberley, 647 miles, at 10.15 P.M. on
the next day, November 1 ; at Mafeking, 870
miles, at 3.12 P.M. on November 2 ; Palachwe, in
Khama's country, 1132 miles, at 12.47 P.M.,
November 3 ; and at Bulawayo, 1360 miles, at
9.30 A.M. on November 4, which would be ninety
hours at fifteen miles per hour.

It took us an hour to cross the Lowry Strait,
which at no very distant period must have been
covered by sea and separated the Cape Peninsula
from the Continent.

At 5.30 we arrived at the Paarl, 35 miles, a
beautiful place suggestive of Italy with its vineyards, gardens and shrubbery, and lovingly en-
folded by the Drakenstein Range.   With its
groves of fir and eucalyptus, bright sunshine, and
pleasant-faced people, with picturesque mountains
round about, it seemed a most desirable place.

The Paarl Station and others we passed bear
witness to the excellence of Cape railway administration.   The names of the stations were boldly
printed on japanned iron plates, and though the
passage of so many trains crowded with distinguished strangers had drawn large assemblages
of the Colonists, male and female, whites, mulattoes,

and negroes, the cleanliness and orderliness that prevailed were very conspicuous.

A MESSAGE TO MR. LABOUCHERE.

At 6 P.M. we had passed Wellington, 45 miles, which went to prove the rate of travel. This town also drew from us admiring expressions for its picturesque situation in one of the folds of the Drakenstein, for the early summer green of its groves, vineyards, and fields, and its pretty white houses. I thought, as I marked the charming town and its church spires, and the sweet groves around, what a contrast it was to the time when the Hottentot reared his cattle in the valley, and the predatory bushman infested the neighbourhood, and preyed on ground game and goats.

On the platform, among those who welcomed our coming, were a dozen Radical shoemakers lately arrived from Leicester. They charged Colonel Saunderson, M.P., my fellow traveller, with an expressive message to Mr. Labouchere. It is too forcible and inelegant for print, but it admirably illustrates the rapidity with which Radicals become perverted by travel.

Darkness found the train labouring through the mountainous defile of the Hex River. We could see but a loom of the rugged heights on either side, but from all accounts this part of the line is one of the show places which strangers are asked to note.

At daylight we were well on the Karroo, which at first sight was all but a desert. However, we were not long on it before we all took to it kindly. The air was strangely appetising, and we could not help regarding it with benevolence. The engineers who designed the line must have been skilful men, and by the track, as the train curves in and out of narrowing valleys and broadening plains, we are led to suppose that the Continent slopes gently from the interior down to Table Bay. The railway is a surface line, without a single tunnel or any serious cutting. The gradients in some places are stiff, but a single engine finds no difficulty in surmounting them.

At 4 P.M. of November 1 we reached the 458th mile from Cape Town, so that our rate of travel had been nineteen miles the hour. On tolerably level parts our speed, as timed by watch, was thirty miles; stoppages and steep gradients reduce this to nineteen miles.

We were fast asleep by the time we reached Kimberley. Night, and the short pause we made, prevented any correct impressions of the chief city of the Diamond Fields. At half-past six of November 2 we woke up at Taungs, 731 miles. The small stream over which we entered the late Crown Colony of Bechuanaland serves as a frontier line between it and Griqualand.

The Capabilities of Bechuanaland.

The first view of the country reminded me of East Central Africa, and I looked keenly at it to gauge its capabilities.   To a new-comer it would not seem so full of promise as it was to me.   It would appear as a waterless region, and too dry for a man accustomed to green fields and flowing rivers, but I have seen nothing between the immediate neighbourhood of the Missouri River and the Rocky Mountains to surpass it, and each mile we travelled in Bechuanaland confirmed that impression.   Every few miles we crossed dry watercourses ; but, though there was no water in sight, it does not derogate from its value as farm land.   The plateau of Persia is a naked desert compared to it, and yet Persia possesses eight millions of people, and at one time contained double that number.   The prairies of Nebraska, of Colorado, and Kansas are inferior in appearance, and I have seen them in their uninhabited state, but to-day they are remarkable for the growth of their many cities and their magnificent farming estates.   All that is wanted to render Bechuana- land a desirable colony is water, so that every farm might draw irrigating supplies from reservoirs along these numerous watercourses.   For Nature has so disposed the land that anyone with observant eyes may see with what little trouble water could be converted into rich green pastures

and fields bearing weighty grain crops. The track
of the railway runs over broad, almost level,
valleys, hemmed in by masses of elevated land
which have been broken up by ages of torrential
rains, and whose soil has been swept by the floods
over the valleys, naturally leaving the bases of the
mountains higher than the central depression. If a
Persian colonist came here he would say : " How
admirable for my purpose !   I shall begin my
draining ditches or *canauts* from the bases of those
hills and train them down towards the lower parts
of these valleys, by which time I shall have as
many constant and regular running streams as I
have ditches, and my flocks and herds and fields
shall have abundance of the necessary element."
A thousand of such Persians would create thus a
central stream with the surplus water flowing along
the valley, and its borders would become one
continuous grove. As the Persians would do, the
English colonists whose luck it may be to come to
this land may also do, and enrich themselves faster
than by labouring at gold mining.

These dry river-beds, now filled with sand, need
only to have stone dams built across, every few
hundred yards, to provide any number of reservoirs. They have been formed by rushing torrents
which have furrowed the lowlands down to the bed
rock, and the depth and breadth of the river courses
show us what mighty supplies of water are wasted
every year. As the torrents slackened their flow,

they deposited their sediment, and finally filtered through underneath until no water was visible, but by digging down about two feet, it is found in liberal quantities, cool and sweet.

Even the improvident black has discovered what the greenness of the grass shows, that, though water is not visible, it is not far off. At one station the guards told me that they could find plenty of water by an hour's digging, which was a marvel to many of our party. I was told in Khama's territory that Khama, the chief, owned eight hundred thousand head of cattle before the rinderpest made its appearance and reduced his stock by half. If true, and there is no reason to doubt it, it shows what Bechuanaland might become with trifling improvements.

MAFEKING.

Before we came to Vryburg, the continuous valley had broadened out into a prairie, with not a hill in sight. The face of the land was as bare as though ploughed. By 4 P.M. we had come to the 850th mile, showing that the rate during the last twenty-four hours had been sixteen and a third miles an hour. Since Taungs, 731 miles, we had been closely skirting the Transvaal frontier, while to the west of the line lay what was once the mission-field of Livingstone and Moffatt. An hour later we arrived at Mafeking, on the Moloppo

River, a tributary of the Orange River. Mafeking
will always be celebrated in the future as the place
whence Jameson started on his desperate incursion
into the Dutch Republic. The Moloppo River
contains lengthy pools of water along its deepened
course, but the inhabitants of Mafeking are
supplied by copious springs from Montsioa's old
farm. The town lies on the north, or right bank,
and is 870 miles from Cape Town. It is 4194 ft.
above the sea. Already it has been laid out in
broad streets which are planted with trees, and as
these are flourishing they promise to furnish
grateful shade in a few years. Outside of the
town there is not a tree in sight, scarcely a shrub,
and consequently it is more purely a prairie town
than any other. Due east of it lies Pretoria, the
Boer capital, about 180 miles distant, and it may
be when the Boers take broader views of their
duty to South Africa at large, and their own
interests, that they will permit a railway to be
constructed to connect the two towns, in which
case the people of Mafeking cannot fail to profit
by having exits at Delagoa Bay, Durban, and
Cape Town. It will be passing strange also if the
neighbourhood of Mafeking will not be found to
contain some of the minerals for which the
Transvaal is famous. The Malmani Gold Field
is about 50 miles off, and the Zeerust Lead and
Quicksilver Mine but a trifle further. For the
growing of cereals it ought also to be as dis-

tinguished as the neighbouring state, for the soil is of the right colour.

In Khama's Country.

On leaving Mafeking we were in the Bechuanaland Protectorate, a country of even greater promise than the Crown Colony. The next morning (November 3) we were well into Khama's country, 1071 miles from Cape Town. A thin forest of acacia trees, about 20 ft. in height, covered the face of the land. The soil was richly ochreous in colour. The grass was young and of a tender green, and the air cool and refreshing. The railway constructors must have rejoiced on finding so little labour required to perform their contract in this section. By skilfully chosen curves they were enabled to easily surmount any unevenness on the surface, and nothing more was required than to lay the steel sleepers on the ground, cross them with the rails, and add a few spadefuls of earth to complete the railway. The train runs wonderfully smooth and steady, and we experienced less discomfort than on some English trains I know. This is naturally due in a great measure to the slower and safer rate of speed we travel, and the newness of the rolling stock. During the whole day we were not once reminded by any jolt, jar, or swaying, of any imperfections, and our nights were undisturbed by loose play of rails or jumping.

At Three Sisters, 388 miles from Cape Town,

we were at the highest altitude of the line, being
4518 ft. above the sea. Thence to Bulawayo, a
thousand miles, the greatest variation in altitude is
1500 ft. ; but were it not for the Railway Guide we
should never have supposed that the variation was
over 100 ft., so imperceptible are the ascents and
descents of the line.

Magalapye Station (1088 miles) consisted of a
third-class carriage and a goods van laid on three
lengths of rail. We were halted nearly an hour
near the Magalapye River, and learned that we
were sixty miles inside of Khama's country. Improvements are proceeding to make the line more
secure during the torrential season. At present it
descends into the bed of the broad stream of sand,
and here, if anywhere, a smart rainfall would
destroy the line. Consequently, a high embankment has been made, stone piers have been built,
and an iron bridge will span the river at a sufficient
height. Here we heard also that one of the special
trains ahead of us had suffered an accident from
the explosion of an oil engine, which generated the
electric light, resulting in the burning of two men,
one of them badly.

The Magalapye River is one of those sandy
watercourses so common in South Africa. To
provide water for the station a broad ditch was cut
across the sandy course, which was soon filled with
clear and excellent water—enough, in fact, to
supply a small township. It is to be hoped that

all the guests noted this and carried away with them the object lesson.

WHAT WATER STORAGE WOULD DO.

The sight of this suggested to me that there was an opportunity for a genius like Rhodes to do more for South Africa than can be done by the discovery and exploitation of gold fields. A company called the United South African Waterworks might buy land along the principal watercourses, build a series of stone dams across them, clean out the sand between them, and so obtain hundreds of reservoirs for the townships that would certainly be established in their neighbourhood.

Beyond Palachwe (1132 miles) the thorn trees begin to disappear, and leafier woods, which resemble dwarf oak, take their place, though there are few trees higher than twenty feet. The soil is good, however, despite the fact that each dry season the fires destroy the grasses and the loams which are necessary for their nourishment. Most of the stations in this part are mere corrugated iron cottages, or railway carriages, temporarily lent for the housing of the guards.

PAUPERISING THE NATIVE.

At each halting place since arriving in Bechuanaland, we have been made aware how quickly the Englishman's generous disposition serves to teach natives to become beggars. Italy, Switzerland, Egypt, have thus suffered great harm. From Taungs to Palachwe, crowds of stalwart and able-bodied natives of both sexes have flocked around the kitchen-car to beg for bread, meat, and kitchen refuse. It is a novel and amusing sight at present, but in the course of time I fancy this practice of patronising beggars will make a callous and offensive breed that will not easily be put off with words.

At Shashi River, 5 P.M., the three special trains lay close together, because of the difficult gradient leading out of the bed of the river. While the engines assisted the trains up the steep, I came across an impromptu presentation of an address by the Mayor of Cape Town to Mr. Logan, the caterer of the excursion parties. According to what was said, we were all made to believe that we could not have been better served had the first European caterer undertaken the provisioning, to which no one could make objection, and a duly signed testimonial to that effect was presented to that gentleman. The scene, however, seemed odd at unknown Shashi, and strongly illustrated a racial characteristic for speech-making and presentation of testimonials.

NEARING BULAWAYO.

On the morning of November 4 we saw as we looked out of the carriage that the country was

[To face page 16.

A GATHERING OF NATIVES, NEAR WATERWORKS, BULAWAYO.

a continuation of that of the previous day.   It
was still as level, apparently, as a billiard table.
We were drawing near to Bulawayo—were, in
fact, due there about 9 A.M.   We had been led
to expect a more tropical vegetation, but as yet,
though we were only sixty miles off, we saw no
signs of it, but rather a return to the thorn bush
of the Karroo and Southern Bechuanaland.   One
variation we noted, the rocky kopje is more
frequent.   These curious hill-heaps of rock are
remnants of the primeval table-land that rose
above the present face of the country from 100
to 300 feet.   The sight of these curious kopjes
deepened the idea that the seat of the "Killer,"
Lo Bengula, would be found on a high eminence,
protected by a cluster of these kopjes, but we
looked long in vain for such a cluster of hills.
Even the sight of a lordly tree would be welcomed,
for the tame landscape was growing monotonous.
The absence of scenery incidents did not diminish
our friendly sympathies towards Rhodesia, and we
made the most of what was actually visible, the
blue sky, the dwarf trees, the low green herbage
which dotted the ground in the midst of wide
expanses of tawdiness, the burnt grass tussocks,
which we knew would in a few days be covered
as with a carpet of green.   We see the land just
before the season changes, and signs of vivifying
spring approaching are abundant.   A few days
ago the first rains set in.   The last two nights

C

have witnessed a wonderful exhibition of electric display in the heavens, and severe thunderstorms have followed. In another fortnight it is said the plains will have become like a vast garden.

At thirty-five miles from Bulawayo we came to the Matoppo Siding. The engineers stopped for breakfast at a restaurant and boarding house! which was a grass hut 20 feet long. Near by a diminutive zinc hut was called "General Store." Several tarpaulins sheltered various heaps of miscellanea. There a Matabele servant of a fur trader informed us that Lo Bengula was still alive, near the Zambesi, happy with abundance of mealies and cattle, and that any white man approaching his hiding-place would be surely killed, but that if any large number of white men went near him, he would again fly.

At the 1335th mile from Cape Town an accident to the special train ahead of us retarded us four hours. The engine, tender, water tank, and bogie car ran off the track. No one was hurt, fortunately, and by 1 P.M. we were all under way again, though the first lunch we were to have eaten together at Bulawayo was necessarily changed to the first dinner.

At 2.30 we were on the alert to catch a first view of Bulawayo, and at 2.55 P.M. a few stray gleams of white, seen through the thorn bush, were pointed out to us as the capital of Matabeleland. We had passed the famous Matoppo Hills to the right of us, but, excepting for their connection with the late war, there was nothing interesting in them. They consist of a series of these rocky kopjes of no great height, lying close together, mere wrecks of the crest of a great land wave, terrible enough when behind each rocky boulder and crevice a rifleman lies hidden, but peaceful now that the war is over, and the white man has made himself an irremovable home in the land.

SIR A. MILNER AT BULAWAYO.

As was said, we entered Bulawayo a few minutes later, and saw the crude beginnings of a city that must, if all goes well, grow to a great distinction. As a new-comer with but an hour or two's experience of it, I dare not venture upon saying anything more. We heard that the Governor, Sir A. Milner, had already officiated at the ceremony of opening the line, that his speech was not remarkable for any memorable words, that he had given the Victoria Cross to some trooper for gallant conduct in the field. I heard that Sir Alfred had also read a despatch from Mr. Chamberlain, which was to the effect that at the opening of the railway to Bulawayo he was anxious to send a message to the settlers assembled to celebrate the event. He sympathised with their troubles, but he was gratified to think that there was a happier future in store for them. The railway would be a stimulus to every form of enterprise, and would effectually bind the north and south together.

C 2

In the evening the dinner took place at the Palace Hotel, which is a building that does not deserve such a title, as might be inferred from the haste with which it was constructed. Ten days ago, few believed that it would be in a fit state to receive any guests, but we found it sufficiently advanced to house the 400 who have arrived. Some portions of it, especially the reception room, would be no discredit to the best hotel at the Cape. The accounts of what occurred at the banquet, as described by the local reporters, I do not reproduce here, and refer my reader to the next chapter for what I have gathered of value from personal observation.

CHAPTER II.

BULAWAYO, *November* 10, 1897.

"RHODESIA HAS A GREAT AGRICULTURAL
FUTURE BEFORE IT."

THE exploration and the development of Rhodesia
have always been regarded by me with sentimental
interest. Every new advance in this region has
been hailed by me with infinite satisfaction, and no
man regretted more than myself the lapses of the
Founder and Administrator in December, 1895,
which threatened to involve the whole of South
Africa in trouble, and to arrest the progress which
had begun. It appeared for a moment as if
Rhodes and Jameson had relinquished golden
substance for a shadow. It is not in human
capacity to realise from a far distance the truth of
the rumours which came from here respecting the
intrinsic value of the land, and so I came here at a
great inconvenience to myself to verify by actual
observation what had been repeatedly stated. I
have been rewarded for so doing by clear convictions, which, though they may be of no great
value to others, are very satisfactory to myself, and

will for ever remain fixed in my mind, despite all contrary assertions. There was a little speech delivered by Commandant Van Rensburg on Monday night, which, perhaps, will be thought by London editors of no importance, but it was most gratifying to me, inasmuch as I had become possessed with the same ideas. He said that it was generally supposed that without gold Rhodesia could not exist, but he differed from that view, as, he was certain in his own mind, it would remain an important country because of its many agricultural products, its native wood, coal, cement, etc., etc. He had come to the conclusion that Rhodesia was as fit for agriculture as any part of South Africa, though he had been rather doubtful of it before he had seen the land with his own eyes. That is precisely my view. It is natural that the large majority of visitors who have come here to satisfy themselves about the existence of gold in Rhodesia should pay but little attention to what may be seen on the surface ; but those who have done so now know that Rhodesia has a great agricultural future before it.

THE OPENING OF THE BULAWAYO RAILWAY.—
   "FEW EVENTS OF THE CENTURY SURPASS
   IT IN INTEREST AND IMPORTANCE."

Several hundreds of men, eminent in divers professions, have come from England, America, the

Cape, Orange Free State, Natal, Basuto and Zulu
Lands, the Transvaal, Bechuanaland, and Northern
Rhodesia, to celebrate the railway achievement by
which this young Colony has become connected
with the oldest Colony in South Africa. In any
other continent the opening of five hundred miles
of new railway would be fittingly celebrated by the
usual banquet and the after-dinner felicitations of
those directly concerned with it; but in this instance
there are six members of the Imperial Parliament,
the High Commissioner of the Cape, the Governor
of Natal, scores of members of the Colonial Legis-
latures, and scores of notabilities, leaders of
thought and action, bankers, merchants, and clergy
from every colony and state in the southern part of
this continent.   They all felt it to be a great event.
Few events of the century surpass it in interest and
importance. It marks the conclusion of an audacious
enterprise, which less than ten years ago would
have been deemed impossible, and only two years
ago as most unlikely.   It furnishes a lesson to all
colonising nations.   It teaches methods of operation never practised before.   It suggests large and
grand possibilities, completely reforms and alters our
judgment with regard to Africa, effaces difficulties
that impeded right views, and infuses a belief
that, once the political and capitalist public realises
what the occasion really signifies, this railway is
but the precursor of many more in this continent.
In fact, we have been publicly told that we are to

expect others, and that the railway to the Victoria
Falls of the Zambesi is the next on the programme.

An Embryo State " Fairly Started into Existence."

The Rudd-Rhodes Concession was granted by
Lo Bengula in 1888. The Charter to the South
Africa Company was given in 1889 ; possession of
Mashonaland was taken by Jameson and his
pioneers on September 12th, 1890 ; Bulawayo was
entered in 1893, and thus the Lo Bengula Concession grew to be Rhodesia. Only four years ago !
But during this brief interval the advance has
been so rapid that, though at home people may
vaguely believe in it, one has to see the town of
Bulawayo and to come in personal contact with its
people to fully comprehend what has been done, and
to rightly understand the situation. With the clearer
view gained by a personal visit the huge map in
the Stock Exchange, which shows the estates,
farms, townships, and mines of Rhodesia, becomes
an encyclopædia of information — the plans of
Bulawayo and Salisbury, and other towns which
have arisen in Rhodesia, valuable directories. If
fresh from an inspection and study of these you
step out and look at the town of Bulawayo, and
glance at the country, you begin to share the
local knowledge of the inhabitants, see with their
eyes, understand on what they base their hopes,

and grasp the real meaning of pushing a railway 500 miles to reach a town of 3000 people. So that, while at home men were arguing that the Rudd-Rhodes Concession was valueless, and Rhodesia a fraud, the land was being avidly bought, prospectors had discovered gold reefs, shafts had been sunk, tunnels had been made to get a fair idea of the value of the reefs, a nominal capital of many millions—some say twenty millions, some say double that sum—had been assured for operations, towns had been created with all the comforts suited to new colonists, and the embryo State was fairly started into existence.

"ENORMOUS POSSIBILITIES IN VIEW."

While being instructed in the hopes and ambitions of several of the local people, my knowledge of how other young countries, such as the States, Canada, Australia, had been affected by the extension of the railway into parts as thinly inhabited as Rhodesia, induced me to cast my glance far beyond Rhodesia, that I might see what was likely to be its destiny, whether it was to be a Free State like Orange, self-sufficient and complacent within its own limits, or broadly ambitious like Illinois State, of which Chicago is the heart. Assuming that the energy which has already astonished us be continued, there are enormous possibilities in view. Bulawayo is 1360 miles from

Cape Town, but it is only 1300 miles of land travel
from Cairo, for the rest of the distance may be
made over deep lakes and navigable rivers; it is
but 1300 miles to Mossamedes, in Angola, which
would bring the town within fifteen days from
London; it is only 450 miles from Beira, on the
East Coast, which would give it another port of
entry open to commerce from the Suez Canal,
India, Australia, and New Zealand; it is but 350
miles from N'gami; it must tap British Central
Africa and the southern parts of the Congo State.
That is the position acquired by Bulawayo by the
railway from Cape Town. Chicago, less than 60
years ago, had far less pretensions than this town,
and yet it has now a million and a half of people.
Something of what Chicago has become Bulawayo
may aspire to. The vast coal fields to which the
new railway is to run, the stone, granite, sandstone,
trachyte, the woods, minerals, gold, copper, lead,
and iron, the enormous agricultural area, are
valuable assets which must nourish it to an equal
destiny. Then the Victoria Falls, larger than
Niagara, what mighty electrical power lies stored
there! I merely mention these things hap-hazard
with the view of assisting my readers to understand the significance of these festivities. Many
men will think and meditate on them, and new
confidence, courage, and energy will be begotten
to stimulate them to greater designs and larger
effort.

The Founding of Rhodesia will cause a Re-Shaping of Policies.

But how does the scene at Bulawayo affect the political world ? It seems to me to have great importance for all South African and British politicians for the way it affects Germany, Portugal, the Congo Free State, and Cape Colony. It will cause people to revise their opinions, and to clear their minds of all previous policies. Any influence that Germany may have hoped to exercise on South African politics has received a check by the insuperable barrier that has been created by those slender lines of steel between its South-West African Colony and the Dutch Republics. The Bechuana Crown Colony and Protectorate, through which they run, must receive a percentage of all immigrants to Rhodesia. These last two are far in advance of the German Colony, and each day must see them strengthened, so that they will become formidable obstacles in the way of German aspirations. These colonies lying along the length of the western frontier of the Transvaal State are four times larger than the Transvaal, and their grand stock-raising areas and agricultural plains having now become easily accessible, cannot remain long unoccupied. I fancy, therefore, that the ambition of Germany to rival our claims to the paramountcy will become wholly extinguished

now, and that her thinkers, like wise men, will
prepare their minds for the new problems which
must be met in a not remote future.

THE LESSON FOR PORTUGAL.

The populating of Rhodesia by mixed races of
whites of a superior order to any near it must
exercise the Portuguese, whose territory lies
between Rhodesia and the Indian Ocean. The
iron road leading to it cannot be closed. The
future of the country is no longer doubtful. We
have tested its climate ourselves; we have heard
the general conviction that these lofty plains,
4500 ft. above the sea, suit the constitution of the
white race; we have seen a hundred English
children going from Bulawayo to a picnic to celebrate the arrival of the railway, and assuredly
that would have been impossible on a tropical day
in any other tropical country I know of. We have
seen scores of infants on the streets, in the suburbs,
on the plains outside, in arms, and in perambulators, and they all looked thriving, pink, and happy.
The market of Bulawayo each day shows us
English vegetables fresh from the garden. We
have seen specimens of the cereals. Well, then, it
appears to me certain that there will be a masterful
population in this country before long, which it
would be the height of unwisdom to vex overmuch
with obsolete ordinances and bye-laws such as

obtain in Portuguese Africa, and burdensome taxes and rates on the traffic that must arise as this country grows in wealth and population. It may be hoped that intelligent Portuguese will do all in their power to promote concord and good feeling with their neighbour, to check refractory chiefs from doing anything to disturb the peace, for nothing could make the people of Rhodesia more restless than interruption to traffic, and a sense of insecurity. If they do that the Portuguese territory must become enriched by the neighbourhood of Rhodesia.

Lessons to Northern Neighbours.

The Congo State will doubtless recognise its profit by the advent of the railway to Bulawayo and the extension of the line towards its southern borders, and the arrangements of the Government will be such as to ensure respect for boundaries and to teach the native tribes that transgression of such will be dangerous.

The British Government have a valuable object lesson for the development of African colonies. For over two hundred years the West African colonies have been stagnating for lack of such means of communication. They have been unable to utilise their resources. Their natural pretensions to the hinterlands have been grievously curtailed, and what ought to have been British is

now French. Nyasaland has also too long suffered
from Imperial parsimony. The function of government should comprise something more than police
duty or the collection of taxes. The removal of
causes injurious to health and life, and the establishment of communication as required by circumstances of climate, and needful to augment
commerce, are just as urgent as the prevention of
lawlessness and the collection of imposts. The
climate of Nyasaland has slain more valuable men
than the assegais of the Angoni. Against the
latter the Government sent their Sikhs ; against
the former they have done nothing. Many of the
sick colonists might have been saved, if, when
weakened by anæmia, a little railway past the
Shiré Rapids had taken them quickly through the
malarious land. If it be worth while to retain and
administer Nyasaland, it is surely worth while to
supply the population with certain means to send
the fruits of their industry to the world's markets,
and to enable them to receive the necessaries of
existence without endangering their lives in the
effort or risking the loss of their goods. Therefore, to a Government that has shown such dread
of constructing an insignificant railway a hundred
miles in length, the enterprise of the Chartered
Company in constructing one five hundred miles
long—and starting immediately upon an extension
two hundred and twenty miles—at the cost of one
and three-quarter millions, must be exceedingly

stimulative. The antique and barbarous method of porterage should be abolished in every British colony, more especially in tropical colonies, where exposure to sun and rain means death to white and black.

How an Enlightened Transvaal Should View the Spread of Free Institutions in the North.

To the South African Republic it is vitally important to weigh well in what manner the Bulawayo railway will affect her future. The Republic will soon be surrounded by a rampart of steel on three sides and alien land and ocean on the other. From Beira, north of the Republic, a railway will run west to Salisbury, and thence south to Bulawayo and the Cape. With two ways of ingress from the sea a country like Rhodesia—with as good a climate as the Transvaal State, with resources which tend to rapid prosperity, enjoying impartial and liberal laws, just and pure administration, opening its arms widely to the whole world without regard to race, blessed with ample domains and suited to the needs of all classes—must necessarily prove more attractive to all people in search of homes, than a country which only favours Dutch burghers ; and Rhodesia therefore bids fair in a few years to overtake the Republic in population, and even to surpass it. The Boers do not avail themselves of the advantages of their position to that fulness which would make it doubtful whether Rhodesia or the Transvaal offered the most inducements to intending settlers. On the contrary, the common report is that the object of the Boers is to restrict population and reserve the State for Boer progeny. I shall see the country for myself, I hope, and either verify or disprove it. But if true, the attempt to suppress population and growth by restrictions, monopolies, and vexatious ordinances is simple imbecility, as compared to the Chartered Company's policy of stimulating commerce by giving free rein to enterprise, and keeping the paths and gates to its territory freely open to all comers. If there is an intelligent man in the Transvaal, it must be clear to him that the Republic must soon lose the rank among South African States to which she was entitled by her wonderful resources and undoubted advantages; and the only thing that can save her from degradation, neglect, and financial difficulties, is the absorption of that alien population which crowds her cities and clamours for political rights.

THE CAPE AND GERMAN PUSHFULNESS.

Cape Colony, though much is due to it for its support of the Bechuana railway, is not wholly free from the blame of inertness in the past. One cannot look at the map of Africa and miss seeing that extraordinary territory labelled German close

MR. J. W. COLENBRANDER'S RESIDENCE (RHODESIA).

[To face page 32.

to Cape Colony, without being reminded of the obtuseness shown by the Cape democracy. But the Germans are a great nation, rich, commerce-loving, and enterprising, and the Cape people need to be warned, considering that they are largely mixed up with Dutch Boers who are slow to move and sadly behind the times. If the Germans chose to invest £4,000,000 in railways from the mouth of the Swakop to the banks of the Orange, they would be formidable competitors for the trade of Bechuanaland and the north of the colony, and Swakop is three days nearer Europe than Table Bay. The railways in America created cities and filled the wastes with settlers, and every new settler was supposed to be worth £200 to the nation ; and in that country they have a mile of railway to every twenty square miles of country. The Cape has but a mile of railway to every 112 square miles. The railways should spread out like a fan from Cape Town. The existing lines require straightening greatly. It is not good policy that the line to Natal should run through alien States, nor is it conducive to the development of the Colony. Some railways may not show large dividends, but they are indispensable to develop-ment and communication : they give value to acres which otherwise would be worthless, and indirectly contribute to revenue in other ways than by dividends. Hence Cape Colony may learn a good deal from this new railway.

Bulawayo reminds Mr. Stanley of Winnipeg.

I think I have said enough to illustrate the position in which Bulawayo has been placed by the arrival of the railway. At present its broad avenues and streets give one an idea that it has made too much of itself. When the avenues are about 90 feet wide and the streets 130 feet wide, naturally the corrugated iron one-storeyed cottages and the one-storeyed brick buildings appear very diminutive ; and the truth is that, were the streets of proportionate width to the height of the buildings, the town would appear very small. The plain upon which it stands gives an idea of infinity that renders poor one-storeyed Bulawayo very finite-looking indeed. The town, however, has laid itself out for future greatness, and the designers of it have been wise. Winnipeg, in Manitoba, which Bulawayo reminds me of by the surrounding plain, was laid out on just such a spacious plan ; but ten years later six-storeyed buildings usurped the place of the isolated iron hut and cottage, and the streets were seen to be no whit too wide. Ten years hence Bulawayo will aspire higher towards the sky, and when the electric trams run in double lines between rows of shade trees, there will be no sense of disproportion between buildings and streets. On the walls of the Stock Exchange I found hanging plans and elevations of the brick and stone buildings already contracted for. They are not to be very lofty, none over two storeys, but architecturally they are most attractive. These new buildings will, perhaps, stand for about five years, for, according to my experience, it is not until the tenth year that the double storey becomes the fashion. At the twentieth year begins the triple storey ; at thirty years the fourth storey begins to appear.

East of the town area devoted to commerce is a broad strip of park. It occupies a gentle hollow in the plain, watered by a crooked ditch, called spruit here, running through a rich, dark, and very thirsty earth. It contains a few puddles here and there along its course. Only a portion of the park is laid out as yet, and that has been well and carefully done. Its plots contain a few hundreds of grape vines, which look like currant bushes. There are also about a hundred very young orange trees, a few flowers, shrubs, etc. A stone column to the memory of Captain Lendy occupies an eminence in it. The whole park has a sombre appearance, owing to the dark soil and ironstone freely sprinkling it. But as the bushes, shrubs, and flowers have only been lately planted, and as around the forcing houses there is a large number of young plants in tins and pots, soon to be transplanted, a couple of years will make an immense difference in the appearance of the pleasaunce.

Beyond and east of the park is the residential part of Bulawayo, divided into two avenues and nine streets running east and west, and eight roads running north and south, named respectively Townsend, Lawley, Livingstone, Pauling, Clark, Duncan, and Heyman, and Park Road, parallel with the park.

Prices of Property and Stands in Bulawayo.

Messrs. Adcock and Norton have furnished me with the prices of stands, or town lots, obtained by them during the last six months. The most noteworthy are Lot 708, with large wood and iron house, £1900; Lot 234, southern half only, bought by Curtis and Co., outfitters, Johannesburg, £3500; Lot 239, half only, bought by Gowie and Co., seedsmen, of Grahamstown, £2000; Lots 451–452 bought by a London firm, £3000; Lot 333, bought by Stuart Campbell and Co., merchants, Johannesburg, £2000; eastern half of Lot 133, 70 feet frontage, on 8th Avenue, purchased by Hepworths, manufacturers, Leeds, England, and South Africa, £5000; Lot 346, corner portion, bought by Knight and Co., boot and shoe makers, Grahamstown, £3600.

HOTEL LIFE AT BULAWAYO.

From various people I have learned that the average estimate of the population is 3000 whites, one-fifth of whom are women and children. There are several hotels, the best of which are the Palace, Maxim, and Charter; but none of them are fit for ladies, and scarcely for gentlemen. The noise and clatter at these forbid sleep, except between midnight and 5 A.M. The food is somewhat coarse, but plentiful; the tea and coffee such as one may obtain on a Cape liner—that is, too strong an infusion of one, and a watery decoction of the other. The cooks evidently are common ship-cooks, as one may gather by the way they boil potatoes and cabbages. The bread is good, the butter is tolerable, the meat is like leather. The waiters, though civil and willing enough, are awkward and new to their work. Board and lodging may be obtained for from £14 to £18 per month, two beds in a room 12 ft. by 12 ft. At the cheaper boarding-houses it will cost between £4 and £10. The rent of lodgings in a small room amounts to 15s. per week.

PRICES OF LIVING AND WAGES AT BULAWAYO.

Prices are likely to be much lower shortly. At present tea is 3s. per lb., coffee 2s. 6d., rice 10d per lb., fresh meat 1s. 6d., corned beef 3s. per tin of 2 lbs., flour 6*d.* per lb., soap per bar 1*s.* 6*d.*, fresh butter 7*s.* to 8*s.* per lb., sugar 1*s.*, matches 1*d.* per box, eggs 15*s.* to 18*s.* per dozen, candles 3*d.* each, fowls 5*s.* each, potatoes 160 lb. for £4 ; vegetables dear.

Wages are high, as might be supposed. Masons and bricklayers obtain 30*s.* per day, tailors 35*s.* per day, carpenters 25*s.* to 30*s.* per day, compositors £9 per week, plumbers and painters £9 per week, waiters, £12 to £15 per month, clerks, first-class, £35 per month, ordinary clerks, £15 to £25 per month, white labourers, 5*s.* per day, black labourers from 1*s.* 3*d.* to 2*s.* per day. The Government lately gave eighty white labourers work on the park at 5*s.* per day to keep them from starvation.

BULAWAYO'S BUILDINGS AND INSTITUTIONS.

The finest buildings of Bulawayo are, first, the long, low building occupied by the Stock Exchange, Telegraph, and Post Office, the Bulawayo Club building, which is extremely comfortable, Sauer's Chambers, and the Palace Hotel, the latter being incomplete ; when finished commercial travellers will, no doubt, find it comfortable, and it may be suitable for ladies.

There are two daily papers, the *Bulawayo Chronicle* and *Matabele Times*, sold at 3*d.* per copy. I have also seen the *Rhodesia Review*, which is, I believe, a weekly issue. There are seven churches—the Wesleyan, Congregational, Church of England, Dutch Reformed, Presbyterian, and Roman Catholic, and one Temperance Hall. There is, of course, a gaol, a fire brigade, and police station. In the gaol are several prisoners, white and black. The crimes of the whites have been burglary, theft, and drunkenness. Among the blacks are fourteen prisoners under sentence of death.

The railway station is fairly adapted for its purpose, though its construction was, necessarily, rapid. The settling reservoirs, fed by pipes from the dams, are not far from it; but I fear that they will be of little use, as the soil is too porous. A coating of cement would make them effective, but the general opinion is that cement would be too costly.

BULAWAYO'S GREAT DEFECT.—BETTER WATER SUPPLY IMPERATIVE.

The great defect of Bulawayo is the smallness of the water supply and the badness of it. At present the inhabitants depend on wells, and water is easily obtainable at 30 and 40 ft., but the water is of a hard and indifferent quality. Up on the Maatschesmuslopje stream, about two and a half miles from the town, there have been constructed three dams of different lengths and varying heights. No. 1 dam is the nearest to Bulawayo, and has a

solid stone and cement core starting from the bed-
rock 10 ft. wide, and decreasing by set-backs of
6 in. to a width of 2 ft. at the top. No. 2 dam
has a puddled core of clay faced with stone, and
No. 3 is of similar construction. In April last
these dams were full and overflowing, but, unfortunately, through bad construction and want of
care, there were several leaks, and it is now
decided to demolish two of the dams and rebuild
them. Nos. 2 and 3 are quite fit to retain the
water catchment, and No. 1 will be finished by the
end of the year. The estimated storage of water
by the three dams is calculated to be between
40 and 45 million gallons. A fourth dam, about
to be erected, will, it is thought, considerably
increase the storage.

Several critics are of the opinion that the dams
will not retain any water, though they were full
last April.

We have had four copious showers of rain since
our arrival on the 4th inst., but a few hours later
the spruits, gullies, and watercourses were almost
waterless, the streets showing scarcely a trace of
the rain, so porous and thirsty is the soil. Daily
it becomes apparent to me that the inhabitants of
Bulawayo should lose no time in studying the art
of water conservation. In a country just within
the tropics an abundant supply of water is essential, and thirty gallons per head per day would not
be excessive. Ten thousand inhabitants should be

[*To face page* 40.

GOVERNMENT HOUSE, BULAWAYO.

(BUILT ON THE SITE OF LO BENGULA'S OLD KRAAL.)

able to command 300,000 gallons daily, but
Bulawayo within twenty years will have probably
20,000, and there is no river between here and
Khama's country that could supply 600,000 gallons
daily. Numbers of little watersheds may be
drained into reservoirs, but if I were a citizen of
Bulawayo my anxiety would be mainly on the
subject of water. The water question is not at all
an insoluble one, because, for the matter of that,
Bulawayo will have always the Zambesi tributaries
to fall back upon, especially the Guay River.

LO BEN'S KRAAL.

At the north end of the town we come to a gate
leading to an avenue which ran perfectly straight
for two miles and a half. The carriage road,
which it is intended to macadamise, is about 30 ft.
wide, and running parallel with it on either side is
an enclosure 50 ft. wide, to be planted with shade
trees. Thus the avenue embraces a width of about
130 ft. At the extremity of it is the Government
House, standing in grounds which four years ago
were occupied by Lo Bengula's kraal. We were
all curious to see the place, and one of the first
objects shown to us was the small tree under which
the Matabele king dispensed his bloody judgments.
Here is a description of the place from
"Zambesia": "The King's capital stands upon a
ridge on the northern side of the Bulawayo River,

in a most commanding position, overlooking as it does the entire country round. Every yard of the ground was covered with dung, layer after layer; the whole place was filthily dirty. The King used to sit on a block of wood in the middle of a great pole stockade, surrounded by sheep and goats."

The first sentence is most misleading, though not inaccurate. The kraal stood upon the same level as the plain of New Bulawayo, but the " Bulawayo River "—a dry watercourse most of the year—has scoured out a broad hollow to a depth of about 20 ft. in the plain, and, as the kraal was seated on the brow above it, it enables one to have a view of a circle of about fifteen miles in diameter, within which are probably three or four of these long, broad swells of plain land.

Government House is a long, low, white-washed house, in Dutch Colonial style, with a pillared verandah outside. It is the property of Mr. Rhodes, as well as the avenue just mentioned. I am told he possesses about eighty square miles altogether hereabouts, and, by the way he is developing his estates, it will some day be a beautiful as well as valuable property.

From Cape Town to Bulawayo Mr. Rhodes Spoken of "With Unqualified Admira- tion."

This reminds me that I have not once mentioned Rhodes, though when describing Rhodesia one

ought not to omit his name ; but the fact is he has
preferred to remain in the veld rather than undergo
the fatigue of the banquets and ceremonies.   From
Cape Town here many men have spoken of him to
me, and always with unqualified admiration.   I
know no man who occupies such a place in men's
thoughts.   His absence has given rise to all kinds
of conjectures as to the cause of it.   Some say it
is due to the fact that the Cape elections are
approaching, and he did not wish to be forced to
a pronouncement of policy ; others that it is due
to Dr. Jameson's zealous care of his health, as he
suffers from heart complaint ; others again say it is
due to a wounded spirit, which too long grieving
might easily end in a Timonian moroseness.
Whatever the true cause may be, he has so
planted himself in the affections of the people that
no eccentricity of his can detract from his merits.
When a man scatters £200,000 a year on the
country out of which he made his wealth, it covers
a multitude of sins in the minds of the recipients of
his gratuitous favours.

> " He does mad and fantastic execution
> Engaging and redeeming of himself,
> With such a careless face and forceless care,
> As if that luck, in very spite of cunning,
> Bade him win all."

The festivities of the celebration end to-night,
or rather to-morrow morning at 1 A.M., and then

Bulawayo will be left to itself to begin its own
proper work of development. We have seen what
Bulawayo is as it terminated the employment of
the ox-wagon, and had just emerged out of the
sore troubles caused by war, famine, and rinderpest.
The next train that arrives after our departure will
be the beginning of a new era. The machinery
that litters the road will be brought up, and the
ox-wagons drawn by fourteen oxen, and the
wagons drawn by twelve mules, and those drawn
by twenty donkeys, will haul it to the mines, and
hence we may hope at the end of a year or so that
Rhodesia will have proved by its gold output its
intrinsic value as a gold field. In my next letter
I mean to touch upon this subject.

CHAPTER III.

BULAWAYO, *November* 11, 1897.

THE NEW ERA IN RHODESIA.

THE festivities are over, and the guests are departing. For seven days we have been entertained as well as the resources of Bulawayo would admit, and the Administrator and Committee have been continuously unflagging in their attentions to us. Next Monday the trains and railway will be occupied in bringing stores and machinery and cattle to supply the needs of the mining industry, and henceforward the traffic will be ordinary and uninterrupted between Cape Town and Bulawayo. On Monday morning also every Bulawayan intends to resume his own proper work, and I suppose that should be the real date of the beginning of the new era in Rhodesia.

WHAT IS RHODESIA?

And here, it seems to me, is a fitting place to ask : What is Rhodesia, about which so much has been said and written ? What are its prospects ? I cannot help but wish I were more qualified by local and technical knowledge to describe the country; but as I have been at some trouble in soliciting the judgment of experienced men, conscientiously weighing the merits of what was told me, and carefully considering what I have personally seen, I can only hope the following summary may have some value to those interested in Rhodesia.

THE LAND TO THE NORTH.

I have been asked by my fellow guests at Bulawayo how the face of the country appeared as compared with the tropical regions further north with which I am more familiar. With regard to the superficial aspect of Rhodesia, I see but little difference between it and East Central Africa, and the southern portion of the Congo basin. Indeed, I am much struck with the uniformity of Inner Africa on the whole. Except in the neighbourhood of the great lakes, which mark the results of volcanic action, where great subsidences have occurred, and the great plains have been wrinkled up or heaved into mountains of great height, the body of Inner Africa away from the coasts is very much alike. The main difference is due to latitude. From the Cape Peninsula to north of Salisbury, or the Victoria Falls, the whole country is one continuous plain country. Between the tops of the highest hills and the highest grassy ridge in the Transvaal the difference of altitude seems solely due to the action of the rain. In the Zambesi basin you have a great shallow basin, and directly you cross the river and travel northward the ascent is being made to reach the crest of the watershed between the Zambesi and the Congo, which is but little higher than the highest grassy ridge in the neighbourhood of Salisbury. From thence a gradual descent is made to reach the central depression of the Congo basin. Northward of the Congo watershed, you gain the average altitudes of the grassy ridges of South Africa, and then begin a descent into the basin of the Tchad Lake, and from thence to the Mediterranean the same system of great land waves rolling and subsiding continues.

NOBLE TIMBER IN RHODESIA.

Latitude—and I might say altitude—however, changes the appearance of the land. Rarely on the tableland of Equatorial Africa do we see the scrub and thorn trees of South Africa. The vegetation there is more robust, the trees taller, the leafage thicker and of a darker green; the mere grasses of the tropics are taller than the trees growing on the plains of Cape Colony, Bechuanaland, and Rhodesia, though in the latter country there are oases favourable to the growth of noble timber. In nitrous belts—fortunately of

no great width—in Ugogo, Nyasaland, East Africa,
we should be reminded of the thorny productions
of Bechuanaland, and ten degrees north of the
Equator we should again see a recurrence of them.

A Magnificent Forest of Teak.

It must have struck even the most unobservant
of our guests how the land improved as we travelled
northward.   How the ungrateful looking Karroo of
Cape Colony was presently followed by expansive
plains covered with dwarf shrubs ; how the plains
became more promising after we passed the Hart
River : how the rolling grassy prairie-like country
of Southern Bechuana was followed by the acacias
and mimosas of Northern Bechuana ; and how as
we neared Rhodesia these trees in a few hours of
travel rose from 10 ft. to 20 ft. in height ; how the
land became more compact, and lost much of its
loose porous texture, and consequently the grasses
were higher and water might be found at a lesser
depth.   That improvement, I am told, continues as
we go northward towards Salisbury, even though
we may keep on a somewhat uniform level, that is
on the tableland separating the river flowing east-
ward, south to the Limpopo and north-west to the
Zambesi.   So rapid is the effect of a lower altitude,
and consequent greater heat and moisture, that
about 80 miles from Bulawayo to the north-west a
magnificent forest of teak has been found, from

MATABELE CHIEFS IN COUNCIL, AT BULAWAYO.

[*To face page* 48.

whose grand timber we saw several specimens of furniture, such as tables, desks, and bureaus, a log of 20 ft. long and a foot square, besides a quantity of planks.

Rhodesia's Fine Climate.

Now, this Rhodesia consists of Matabeleland and Mashonaland, and covers about a quarter of a million square miles. It is the northern portion of the Great South African tableland, and its highest elevations run N.E. and S.W., varying from 4000 to nearly 6000 feet above the sea. This height declines on the eastern, southern, and north-western sides, as it slopes along with the rivers flowing from them. This high land, which is eminently suitable for European families, is about 70,000 square miles in extent, of solid, unbroken agricultural country as compared with Ireland, Scotland, and Wales. Those who remember what countries of similar superficial area in Europe can contain in population may be able to gauge what numbers of the white race may exist in Rhodesia. Outside the limit I have mentioned the resident must expect to be afflicted with malarial fevers, and the lower one descends towards the sea, the more frequent and severe will they become. There is this comfort, however, that long before the upper plateau is over-populated, population will have made a large portion of the malarious districts

E

healthy and inhabitable—at least, it has been so found in every land that I have visited. On the upper lands, the resident who has come by way of the Cape and Bechuanaland need have no fear of malaria. I regard my own oft-tried system as a pretty sure indicator of the existence of malaria, for a very few hours' residence in a country subjected to this scourge would soon remind me of my predisposition to it ; but during the whole of the time I have spent in Rhodesia I have not felt the slightest symptom. I have seen white women driving their babies in perambulators on the plain outside Bulawayo in a sun as hot as any in the Egyptian or Moroccan desert, and, though I felt they were unwise, it was clear to me that in such a climate a sufficient head protection was the only thing necessary to guard against a sunstroke or the feverish feeling which naturally follows a rash exposure to heat.

THE RAINY SEASON.

Rhodesia has been visited by us during what is generally said to be its worst period. The rainy season begins in November and ends in March. We arrived November 4, and, though we have been here only a week, we have had four showers and one all-night downpour. The rainfall during the season amounts to as much as 45 in. I fancy few men have had larger experience of the pernicious effects of cold rains alternating with hot suns than I, and the composure of the Bulawayo population under what seems to promise four months of such weather strikes my imagination, and is to me a strong testimony of the healthfulness of the climate.

No Stint of Vegetables.

The park of Bulawayo, the grounds of Government House, and especially the advanced state of Mr. Colenbrander's charming gardens, afforded to me valuable proofs that the soil responded very readily to civilised treatment; but the most conclusive proof to me of the capacity of the soil was furnished by a large market garden laid out in a depression just outside of the town. From end to end the garden, supplied with water by a wind-pump from a well, was a mass of robust European vegetables, whence cabbages weighing 30 lb. each, and tomatoes of extraordinary size, have been sent to market. At the Palace Hotel the hundreds of guests made large demands for vegetables, and there was no stint of them. Further on towards old Gubulawayo we were attracted by native women hoeing in a field, and our attention was drawn to the native fields, which showed by the old corn-stalks that the Matabele must have found the black earth of the plains gracious to their toils. Here and there in these villa gardens, market gardens, public pleasaunces, and ornamental grounds we found sufficient evidences that, given water, the soil of Rhodesia was equal to supplying anything that civilised man with his fastidious taste and appetite could possibly demand.

THE GOLD OF RHODESIA—SOMETHING TO SATISFY AN ANXIOUS MIND.

The next thing to do was to find out something relating to the precious metal, whose presence in Rhodesia was the immediate cause of the railway. I remember last session having heard in the Smoking Room of the House of Commons the most disparaging views regarding the prospects of Rhodesia and the quality of the reefs. The gold of Rhodesia was said to be "pocket" gold, and that the ancients, whose presence long ago in this land is proved by the multitude of old workings and disused shafts, were too clever to have left any for us moderns. Not knowing how to controvert such statements, I had left them unanswered, half believing that they were true. Sir James Sive-wright, in his speech on the first festal night, said that Bulawayo was built upon faith, and the majority of the guests I discovered held the most doubtful views, and I must confess little was needed to confirm the scepticism which had been planted in me in England. But when I heard that there was an exhibition of ores to be seen in the Hall of the Stock Exchange, I felt that the Reception Committee had provided for us something more valuable than banquets—something which should satisfy an anxious mind. Within a well-lighted, decent-sized hall, on an ample shelf ranged around it, a few of the mining companies of Rhodesia had sent various specimens of the ores. Above these shelves hung admirably-drawn maps to illustrate the reefs whence they were taken. I had noticed, as I went in, other specimens of Rhodesian products ranged along the passages— bulky lumps of coal from the Zambesian coal district, a coal that is said to give only from 8 per cent. to 12 per cent. of ash; fine red sandstone blocks, a stone closely resembling that of which most of the houses on Fifth Avenue, New York, are built; blocks of grey sandstone, to which substance I had already been attracted, it being so much used for lintels and doorways of Bulawayan houses; and rough and polished granite blocks, which reminded me of the famous Aberdeen stone, besides several limestone briquettes.

PLENTY OF EVIDENCES OF GOLD.

The first exhibits of ores I happened to inspect were from the Camperdown Reef, in which the virgin gold was conspicuous enough to satisfy the most unbelieving. The next exhibit consisted of a

number of briquettes of cement manufactured in
Bulawayo. The third was a glass case which
contained old gold beads, discovered at Zimbabwe,
and attracted a great deal of attention from the
dusky appearance of the metal which centuries had
given it, the rude workmanship, evidently African,
and the puerility of the ornaments. Beyond this
the Rhodesia Ltd. Company had specimens from the
Criterion Reef, situate eight miles from Bulawayo.
The rock contained no visible gold, and the
Curator who guided me round had the assurance to
say that the quartz where gold was not visible was
more appreciated than that which showed nuggets.
This made me think of the mountains of white
quartz I had seen on the Congo, and to wonder
whether the Curator was indulging in unseemly
levity. However, perceiving some doubt in my
glance, he said it would be demonstrated shortly.
Adjoining the Criterion ores was a heap from the
Nellie Reef in the Insiza district, fifty miles from
Bulawayo. The Curator said these were "very
rich," and taken from old workings; but despite
the Curator and the old workings, I could not see
a trace of gold in the rock, even with a magnifier.
Next to the Nellie exhibit was a pile of rock from
the Unit and Unicorn Reef—in the Selukwe
district, Eastern Rhodesia—but I saw no gold in
any one of these rocks.

A Successful Crushing of Gold Quartz.

Just at this juncture the Curator told me that one of these apparently valueless rocks was about to be crushed and panned for our instruction. We went out into a yard, where there was quite a crowd of curious people assembled. The lump of rock was put into a small iron mortar, and in a few minutes it was pounded into a dusty looking mass. It was then passed through a fine sieve and the larger fragments were returned into the mortar to be again pounded. A sufficient quantity of the greyish dust having been obtained, the mortar was emptied into a broad iron pan. The pan was dipped into a tub full of muddied water, a dexterous turn or twist of the wrist, and the coarser material was emptied into the tub. Frequent dippings and twists reduced the quantity of material in the pan, until at last there was barely a tablespoonful of it left, and still I saw no glitter. Again the dipping and twisting and rinsing were repeated, until at last there was only a teaspoonful of the dirt left; but all around the bottom of the pan was a thin thread of unmistakable gold dust. It was beyond belief that such a barren-looking piece of quartzose rock should contain gold; but then these experts are wonderful fellows. I pay them my most respectful homage.

How the Ancient Miners Worked.

Returning to the Hall under the influence of this
very needful lesson, I resumed my examination of
the exhibits.   Beyond the Unit and Unicorn
exhibit stood some planks of a teaky quality,
beautifully polished, and showing numbers of
small dark knots, and wavy patterns, which gave a
walnuty appearance to the wood.   The next
exhibit was from the Gwanda district by the
Geelong Gold Mining Company, taken from a
90-ft. level.   In this district the ancient workings
are found deepest.   The prehistoric miners were
accustomed to build charcoal fires on the quartz,
and when the rock was sufficiently heated threw
water on it, which soon disintegrated it and
enabled the picks and gads to be used.   This
reminded me how often I had done the same to
huge rocks which blocked the way for my wagons
on the Congo.   The broken quartz, being brought
to the surface, was handed to natives who crushed
it to dust on blocks of granite with diorite
hammers, or ground it as the modern natives do
mealies.   The dust was then panned in much the
same way as is done by prospectors of to-day.   In
one of the old shafts, over 60-ft. deep, was found
the dome of a human skull and some pieces of
human bone.   These relics lay side by side with
the quartz exhibits.   One could moralise here if
one had time.

A GROUP OF ARMED BOERS : CAMP NEAR JOHANNESBURG.

[*To face page* 56.

FINE SPECIMENS OF COAL.

The exhibit of the Ellen Reef of the United Matabele Claims Development Company showed distinct gold. Just near it were blocks of fine-looking coal from the Matabele Gold Reefs and Estates Company. The coal-field is situated 120 miles north of Bulawayo. The coal has been already tested, and is found to be admirable for all uses.

120 OUNCES TO THE TON.

The Nicholson Olympus Block, Gwanda district, showed specimens which panned 120 oz. to the ton. The Mary Reef specimens assayed 5 oz. 3 dwt. 10 gr. to the ton. Next to these was a clock frame made out of trachyte in the form of a Greek temple. This trachyte is greyish white in colour and easily workable, but hardens by exposure. As there is plenty of this material it is probable Bulawayo will make free use of it in future. Mansions and villas of this stone would look extremely chaste and beautiful.

THE TEBEKWE MINE.

Then we came to the exhibits from the Tebekwe Mine, Selukwe district, seventy miles from Bula-wayo on the Salisbury Road. The large map above was worth studying. It illustrated a reef about 1100 yds. in length, and eight oval-form excavations made by the ancients resembling the pits Kimberley diamond diggers formerly made in the blue clay. The base lines of these excavations were not much over 60 ft. from the surface. On the appearance of water in each shaft the ancients were unable to make their fire on the exposed quartz reef, and consequently had to abandon it, and they probably made another excavation along the reef until the appearance of water compelled them to relinquish that also. 900 yds. of this reef have now been proved by means of twelve winzes, the majority of which have been sunk to the first level 154 ft. below the surface. On this first level 887 ft. of driving has been done up to the present. The second level is 234 ft. below the surface, and three winzes have been sunk to it. The total footage to now made is 3,311 ft. 10 in. The average width of the reef is 41½ in., and the narrowest width is 15 in. Throughout the mine the average width is 31 in. I am told that the richest average value of the reef is 84 dwt. per ton of 2000 lb., and the poorest 5 dwt. to the ton. Throughout the reef averages 17·73 dwt. of fine gold per ton ; 12 dwt. is considered a payable quantity at Bulawayo. A block of rock from the centre shaft showed 57 dwt. to the ton.

A twenty-stamp battery is on the rails between Port Elizabeth and Bulawayo, beside steam hauling gear and electric pumping machinery, and it is anticipated that the mine will be in operation about October, 1898.

"THE BEST MINES IN RHODESIA."

I next came to the Gaikwa and Chicago Reef, whose old workings had a shaft 70 ft. deep. Its present owners sunk this to 100 ft. when they came to the abandoned reef. I think the assay showed 1 oz. 11 dwt. to the ton.

Close to it were specimens from the Adventurers Reef in the Insiza district which assay 1 oz. to the ton. Beyond was the Willoughby's Consolidated Company, Limited, which had exhibits from the favourite mines, called Bonsor, Dunraven, and Queen's. Shafts in the Bonsor have been sunk to 365 ft., the lode is 30 in. wide, and the average assay per ton is 18 dwt. The Dunraven has been sunk to a depth of 320 ft., lode and assay the same as the Bonsor. The Queen's has been penetrated 100 ft., lode 30 in., and assay 18 dwt. People who have no pecuniary interest in mines have told me that the best mines in Rhodesia, and of which there is not the least doubt, are the Globe and Phœnix, Bonsor, Dunraven, Tebekwe, and Geelong, all of which are in the Selukwe district, excepting the last, which is in Gwanda.

Next were exhibits from the Matabele Sheba Gold Mining Company : dark quartz, of which there were fourteen specimens. This reef is twenty miles

from Bulawayo, and assays 2 oz. 10 dwt. per ton.
The Marlborough Reef, four miles from Bulawayo ;
the Ullswater Reef, sixteen miles from town ;
Piper's Reef, three miles from town, averaging
respectively 1 oz. to 5 oz., 15 dwt. to 5 oz., and
25 dwt. Very little gold is visible in these specimens ; but the owners have panned repeatedly,
and are satisfied that they contain the precious
metal in profitable quantities.

Bulawayo the Centre of Auriferous Fields.

Just above these specimens was a large map
showing the Rhodesian Gold Fields very clearly.
From this I learned that the Gwanda district was
south of Bulawayo ; the Tuli district, which contains the Monarch Mine, is south-west from here,
and constitutes a little republic of its own ; the
Bembezi field is north ; Insiza district is east ; and
so is the Filabusi and Belingwe ; the Selukwe
district is E.N.E., comprising Gwelo ; the Sebakwe,
N.E. ; and the Mafungabusi district, N.N.E. ; so
that the Bulawayan gold field seems to be the
centre of this cluster of auriferous fields.

The Fort Victoria exhibit showed a large lump
of native copper and excellent bits of gold quartz.
The Masterton Reef, forty miles from Bulawayo,
had two specimens and certificate of assay of
18 dwt. and 22 dwt. respectively.   The Springs

Reef, Belingwe district, exhibits consisted of galena, copper and gold, and appeared very fine.

THE UNRELIABILITY OF ASSAYS.

From the No. 2 Kirkcubbin Reef, Bulawayo district, it appeared that an assay of 62 oz. 16 dwt. to the ton was obtained, while from the No. 1 same reef there was an assay of 24 oz. 14 dwt. to the ton. It should be observed that these assays, no matter by whom they are made, are misleading to the uninitiated, and though the panning is better, neither are to be relied on as sure guides to what the reef will prove throughout. When, say, 10,000 tons are crushed we shall better know by the result the true status of Rhodesia among gold-bearing countries. Nevertheless, every assay or panning has a value as indicating the presence of gold.

The next exhibit was from the Sinnanombi gold belt, south of the Matoppos. The St. Helen's Development Syndicate exhibit consisted of several pans full of grey powdered quartz ready for panning, each of which has been assayed by the Standard Bank with the following results: Thirkleby, Antelope, Rosebery, Constitution and Thela Reefs, in the Sinnanombi district, respectively 2 oz. 4 dwt., 136 dwt., 27 dwt. 18 gr., 58 dwt., and 46 dwt. The Syndicate have also properties in the Insiza district, the Nellie Rey Reef, Eileen Reef in Mavin district, Ben Nevis and Guinea Fowl Reefs in Selukwe district.

"In Every Stone the Gold Sparkled."

The West Glen May Mine exhibit contained sections, one of which was remarkable as showing a 60-ft. wide reef. Its rock specimens were rich with visible gold. There was also a rich exhibit from the Christmas Reef, sixteen miles from Bulawayo—in every stone the gold sparkled.

From Purdon's Reef, in the Makukuku district, alluvial gold was on show. There was also an old iron gad from the ancient workings. Alluvial gold is found in the Myema River, twenty miles from Bulawayo.

Among other things at the Chamber of Mines Exhibition was a thick log of fine grained teak, several planks, furniture from native woods, samples of lime, trachyte blocks, Bulawayo brick, coal blocks from Tuli coal districts 200 miles S.E. of Bulawayo and the Zambesi district 120 N. of Bulawayo, and a champagne case full of plumbago lately discovered at a spot fifty miles from the Zambesi.

For the patient courtesy shown to me while making my notes, and the instructing and interesting conduct of me round the room, I am under the warmest obligations to Mr. Walter Broad, the Hon. Curator, who, as you will be interested to know, is a Canadian, and whose first impulse to seek Africa as a field for his labours was obtained through reading my "Dark Continent."

A Visit to the Criterion Mine.

After this exhaustive inspection of the ores on exhibition, it remained for us to see one of these Rhodesian mines in operation to dispel the last remnant of doubt which eloquent sceptics had inspired me with. We chose the Criterion Mine, which is by no means the nearest to the town. It belongs to the Rhodesia Ltd. Company, and is situate eight miles south from Bulawayo, and as Mr. Hirschler, the Engineer of the mine, was willing to take upon himself the trouble of being our guide, we flung ourselves gladly upon his generosity. In one hour and a half we made the distance in a spring cart drawn by four spirited little mules. We halted at the Engineer's station on a commanding grassy ridge, which neighbours that once occupied by Mosilikatse's old kraal of Gubulawayo during the forties, fifties, and sixties of this century. A few spaces from the spot where we outspanned we came to a series of "old workings" which ran along the crest of the ridge for about 2000 ft. Where one of these old workings was untouched by the Engineer, it reminded me of just such a big hole as might have been made to unearth a boulder, or to root out a large tree. One of these hollows was chosen by the Engineer to sink his first shaft. After penetrating through fifty feet of débris, he came upon the reef which the ancients

had abandoned because of flooding, and time,
aided by rain, had filled up.   He continued for
about 10 ft. more, sampling every 3 ft. as he went
to discover the grade of the ore.   Since then he
has sunk eight other shafts.   The mine consists of
170 claims, but the development is concentrated
on about twenty-five claims, ten of which are in
the centre of the property, and fifteen towards the
eastern boundary.   In the centre two shafts are
being sunk to the 150 ft. level, and are at present
connected by a drive 300 ft. long.   On this level
the reef is throughout payable, while a chute
100 ft. long is of high grade ore.   Trenches on
the line of the reef indicate its occurrence towards
the eastern portion of the mine, where five shafts
varying from 100 ft. to 150 ft. deep have been
sunk.   At the depth of 150 ft. the various shafts
will be connected by a gallery, which will give
2000 ft. of reef material.   At the present time
work is being done for the purpose of developing
sufficient ore to keep a 20-stamp mill going.   The
necessary machinery has been ordered, and the
engineers expect to begin producing some time
about the middle of 1898.   On examining the
material at the mouths of the shafts, those among
us who knew of what they were speaking declared
that much of it was of high grade.   High pyritic
quartz abounded, and this was rich in fine gold.
Sulphide galena was found in some of the quartz.
At the mouth of one shaft visible gold was very

frequent, and about forty of the visitors obtained specimens wherein miniature nuggets were plainly visible. Where the reef was being worked at the deepest shaft it showed a breadth of 24 in. ; in some places it is only 18 in. wide ; at others it is 48 in. broad.

"WE SAW ENOUGH TO PROVE THAT RHODESIA IS AN AURIFEROUS COUNTRY."

My readers need scarcely be told that the exhibits of ores are only such as a few companies of Rhodesia were induced to send after urgent appeals from the public-spirited citizens of Bulawayo. I saw none from Salisbury, Mazoe, or any part of Mashonaland, and only a few mines in Matabeleland were represented. There was no time for a proper exhibition. Many more were *en route*, but the distances are great and the ox-wagon is slow. At any rate we have seen sufficient to prove that Rhodesia is an auriferous country though as yet no one knows what rank it will take among gold-producing lands. My own conviction —a conviction that is, I suppose, made up from what I have seen and heard from qualified men— is that Rhodesia will not be much inferior to the Transvaal. True, it has no Witwatersrand—forty miles of reefs ; but the superficial area is twice the size of the Transvaal State, and the prospectors have only succeeded in discovering a few plums.

F

Then, though the railway has been brought to
Bulawayo, it is still far from the Belingwe and
Selukwe districts, and within a radius of 100 miles
from the town there are many gold fields richer
than those in the immediate neighbourhood of the
railway terminus. It is necessary to state this in
the clearest manner, for many will be carried away
by the idea that now the railway is at Bulawayo
the output of gold should follow immediately.
But even the most forward among the mining
companies can only say: "We have ordered all
the needful machinery and shall set to work as
soon as it arrives." The machinery in a few
cases is on the rail between Port Elizabeth and
Bulawayo ; but the necessities of life must precede
mining machinery, and several weeks more may
elapse before any portion of the material may
reach Bulawayo. Then we shall have to consider
the terrible calamity endured by Rhodesia, as well
as South Africa in general. The rinderpest is not
over yet, and cattle, mules, and donkeys are scarce,
and the haulage of heavy machinery over the veld
with feeble and sickening cattle for forty, seventy,
and a hundred miles will be a tedious business.
Then will come the erection of buildings, the
fitting of engines, etc., etc., with inexpert natives,
and I think I need but suggest that all these
preliminaries will occupy much time. The more
confident engineers declare that they will be ready
to produce about the middle of next year. They

may be as good as their word, knowing their business better than we casual visitors ; but it seems to me but common prudence to withhold expectation of results until eighteen months from the present.

RHODESIA'S REQUIREMENTS.

There is no doubt in my mind that gold will be produced in payable quantities from these Rhodesian mines ; but the extent of profit depends upon circumstances. It is also as certain that Rhodesia cannot hope to compete with the Transvaal under present conditions. Bulawayo is 1360 miles from the sea, and at least 40 miles from the richest mines. Johannesburg is 390 miles from the sea, and is in the centre of its forty mile long gold field. That simple fact means a great deal, and shows an enormous disadvantage to Rhodesia. The latter country will have to pay four times more for freight than the Transvaal gold fields. Against this must be set the small duties that will have to be paid. After paying five per cent. to Cape Colony, goods will be admitted free to Rhodesia. Then the heavy taxes paid to the Boers will still further diminish the disadvantages of Rhodesia ; yet when we consider the time wasted in the long railway journey, and the haulage by ox-wagon to the mines, we shall find a much heavier bill of costs against the gold output of Rhodesia, than on that of the Transvaal. A good substantial railway from Beira or Sofala to Bulawayo, *viâ* Victoria, would completely reverse things. Bulawayo would then be about the same rail distance from the sea as Johannesburg is ; the poorer ores could then be worked profitably, and the aggregate of gold product would in a few years rival that of the Rand. If I were a Chartered Director, my first object should be to get the shortest and most direct route to the sea from Bulawayo, and a substantial railway along it, and having obtained that, and a liberal mining law, I should feel that the prosperity of Rhodesia was assured.

CHAPTER IV.

Letter from Johannesburg.

GO-AHEAD BULAWAYO.

BETWEEN Bulawayo and Johannesburg there is a great difference. In common with some 400 guests of the Festivities Committee, I looked in admiring wonderment at the exuberant vitality, the concentrated joyous energy, and the abounding hopefulness of the young sons of British fathers who, in the centre of Rhodesian life, were proud of showing us a portion of their big country, and what they had done towards beginning their new State. We shared with them their pride in their young city, their magnificently broad avenues, the exhibits of their resources, their park, their prize cabbages, and the fine, bold, goaheadiveness which distinguished their fellow-citizens. We felt they had every reason to be proud of their victories over the rebel Matabele, the endurance they had shown under various calamities, and the courageous confidence with which they intended to face the future. From our hearts we wished them all prosperity.

JOHANNESBURG'S WRONGS.

At Johannesburg, however, different feelings possessed us. Without knowing exactly why, we felt that this population, once so favoured by fortune, so exultant and energetic, was in a subdued and despondent mood, and wore a defeated and cowed air. When we timidly inquired as to the cause, we found them labouring under a sense of wrong, and disposed to be querulous and recriminatory. They blamed both Boers and British: the whole civilised world and all but themselves seemed to have been unwise and unjust. They recapitulated without an error of fact the many failures and shames of British Colonial policy in the past, gave valid instances of their distrust of the present policy, pointed to the breaches of the Convention of 1884, and the manifest disregard of them by the Colonial Secretary, described at large the conditions under which they lived, and demanded to know if the manner in which the charter of their liberties was treated was at all compatible with what they had a right to expect under the express stipulations of the Convention. "Why," said they, "between Boer arrogance and British indifference, every condition of that Power of Attorney granted to Paul Kruger has been disregarded by the Boer, and neglected by the British." They then proceeded to dilate upon Boer oppression, Boer corruption, the cant and hypocrisy of President Kruger, the bakshish-begging Raad, the bribe-taking Ministry, the specious way in which promises were made, and, when their trust was won, the heartless way in which these same promises were broken. From these eloquent themes they proceeded to detail their worries from taxation, high wages, extortionate freight charges, the exactions levied upon every necessity of their industry, the exorbitant price for coal, and imposts on food designed expressly to pamper the burgher at the expense of the miner. Then in a more melancholy tone they discussed the mistakes of their friends—Jameson's tactless raid—the poverty of the country, the decline of business in the city, the exodus of the Australians, and the prospects of a deficit in the Treasury, etc., etc.

CONTACT BRINGS CONVICTION.

I wish that I could have taken down verbatim all that was said to me, for the spokesmen were of undoubted ability, fluent in speech, and full of facts, not a tithe of which I can remember. As I fear I cannot do justice to what was urged with such vehemence and detail, you must be content with the broad sense of their remarks only. These men have stories to say which should be said to shorthand writers. I have read many books and articles on South African politics, but I was never so interested or convinced as when these men told their stories straight from the heart.

Johannesburg Early Last Month.

I then turned an inquiring attention to the Johannesburg newspapers, and from a heap of them obtained their opinions on the gloom prevailing in the "Golden City." There were columns of allusions to the general distress, of the unemployed becoming numerous, of tradespeople unable to find custom. Clergymen had been interviewed, who said that "poverty was rampant," that shopkeepers were almost distracted through fear of insolvency, that the country's credit was going and almost gone, that Australians were leaving in such numbers that sufficient berths on steamers could not be found, and that the inaction of the Government was driving skilled and willing workmen away.

Effects of Bad Times.

My hotel-keeper, a bright sociable man, was induced to give me his own opinions on the depression. He acknowledged that his own hotel was doing fairly well, but the other hotels were mostly empty. Tradesmen he knew were bitterly lamenting the want of custom, buildings in course of erection were stopped because the owners

A GROUP OF BOERS ON COMMANDO.

[To face page 72.

did not think themselves justified in proceeding
with the structures, rents were hard to collect from
tenants, the upper storeys were already empty,
reductions had been made on the lower floors, and
still there were no permanent tenants ; goods stored
in bonded warehouses had to be auctioned, as the
proprietors had not the means to take them away,
etc., etc.

ONE MAN'S VIEW ——

Encountering a gentleman whom I knew in
Sydney, Australia, and who is now on the Stock
Exchange here, I inquired of him what he thought
of the condition of things. He said : " Mostly
everything is at a standstill, I think. To-day
stocks and real estate are a trifle firmer, but I
cannot conceive any reason for it. There is
nothing within my knowledge to justify confidence.
Old Kruger is relentless and implacable. He will
never yield, whatever people may say. And unless
the reforms are granted, so that the mines can be
worked at a profit, Johannesburg must decline,
and things will become as bad for the State as for
ourselves. The old man positively hates us, and
would be glad to see the town abandoned. On
the strength of the Industrial Commission report,
many of us bought largely, but when we found
that there was a majority against us, we sold out
in such a haste that for a while it looked like
a panic. The majority in the Raad had been

bought out by the Dynamite Company, and, of course, we were helpless. You people at home have no idea of the corruption of our Government. Kruger appears not to know that when he calls the Dynamite Company a corner-stone of the State, he is giving himself away. We know that the Company and its twin brother, the Netherlands Railway Company, support the twenty-four members of the Raad, and as they, with Kruger, are the State, those companies may well be called corner-stones."

AND ANOTHER'S.

At the club I met a gentleman whose moderate way of expressing himself made me regard him as being inclined to be impartial, and when urged to give his views, he said that "undoubtedly there were great grievances which every well-wisher of the State would desire to see removed. The administration was so corrupt that it was difficult to get a Boer official to attend to any business, unless his palm was oiled beforehand. The officials had got into the habit of excusing themselves from doing their duties because they were overwhelmed with work, or that they had no time. It is a way they have of hinting that unless it is made worth their while, they will not put themselves out to do what they are paid to do by Government. Many companies understand this so well that they set apart a fund from the profits to meet this necessity. You know, perhaps, that the Dynamite Concession is one of the most corrupt things in the State. One member of the Raad gets five shillings a case, and the Government pocket ten shillings for every case of dynamite sold in the Republic. When we know that forty-seven shillings would be a sufficient price for a case of dynamite, to invoice a case at forty shillings higher shows that some people must have grand pickings. Were the mines in full operation they would consume about 250,000 cases, and this extortion of £2 a case means £500,000 blackmail on the mining industry. Then the railway administration is just as bad. The tariff is abnormally heavy. The first-class fares are greatly in excess, and as for freight charges, you can imagine how high they were when it was proved during the drift closure that ox-wagons could make the transport as cheaply as the railway."

"Then you appear to justify Rhodes in his attempt to. rectify this?" I said.

"No, I do not; but all that he stated before the Parliamentary Committee about the abuses is perfectly true. I cannot, however, absolve him for attempting to promote a revolution to effect a change. But about this corruption at Pretoria. I do not blame the Boers so much as I blame the Hollanders and our Jews here. They are the real causes of the disorders in the State. The corruption was started by the Hollanders, and the

Jews have been only too willing to resort to bribery, until the share market has become demoralised. These fellows unite together to discredit a mine, until there is no option but to close it. Many of the mines have been closed through their intrigues. Mine is one of them, for instance."

PASSING CUSTOMS AT VEREENIGING.

This was my first day's introduction to the moral condition of Johannesburg. But to begin at the beginning. On arriving at midnight at the frontier of the Transvaal, near the Vaal River, the train was stopped in the open veld until daylight, for Boer officials require daylight to make their conscientious examination of passengers and their luggage. Half-an-hour after dawn the train moved over the Vaal Bridge, and we were soon within the grip of the Boer Custom House. I was told later that the officials were insolent; but I saw nothing uncommon, except a methodical procedure such as might belong to a people resolved to make a more than usually thorough search. The officials came in at the rear end of the carriage, locked the door behind them, and informed us we were to go out before them. The male passengers were ushered into one corrugated-iron house, the females with their respective searchers behind them into another. One burly passenger had diamonds concealed on his person, but his clothes were only slightly felt. A small pale clergyman just behind him, however, received marked attention, and was obliged to take off his boots, and every article of his baggage was minutely scrutinised. Probably some of the women searchers performed their duties just as thoroughly. My servant was asked to pay duty on some of my shirts, but he refused to pay anything, on the ground that the shirts had been repeatedly worn and washed.

GETTING NEWS FROM THE RAND.

The distance to Johannesburg from the frontier was but an hour and a half of ordinary running, but from the time we neared the Vaal River it occupied us eleven hours. A reporter from the *Star* had come aboard at the frontier station, and from him we learned a few facts regarding Johannesburg, such as that the uitlander miners intended to starve the burghers out by closing the mines, that the Australians were leaving in crowds, and though there were three Presidential candidates in the field, Kruger was sure to be returned for a fourth term, as General Joubert was known to be weak, and Schalk Burger almost unknown.

A PANORAMIC VIEW OF THE MINES.

The Transvaal veld was much greener, and more rolling, than that of the Orange Free State.

Johannesburg came into view about 9 A.M.; but instead of making direct for it, the train sheered off and came to a halt at Elandsfontein, six miles east. It was then we first obtained an intelligent comprehension of the term "Main Reef," to whose production of gold the existence of Johannesburg is due. Its total length, I am told, is 38·5 miles, to be accurate, and along this a chain of mines, well equipped and developed, exists, out of which, however, only ten miles of the reef can be profitably worked under the present economic circumstances. The working of the remaining twenty-eight miles depends mainly upon the removal of the burdens, upon low wages, abundant labour, cheap transport, etc. The richer and dividend-paying section of the Reef contains such mines as the Langlaagte, Paarl Central, Crown Reef, Pioneer, Bonanza, Robinson, Worcester, Ferreira, Wemmer, Jubilee, City and Suburban, Meyer and Charlton, Wolhuter, George Goch, Henry Nourse, New Heriot, Jumpers, Geldenhuis, Stanhope, and Simmer and Jack. To either side of Elandsfontein runs a lengthy line of chimney stacks, engine houses, tall wooden frames, supporting the headgear, stamp mills, with clusters of sheds, huts and offices, hills of white tailings, and ore. To the westward these become more numerous, and as the train moved from Elandsfontein towards Johannesburg, it clung to the side of a commanding ridge by which we obtained a panoramic view of mine after mine, each

surrounded by its reservoirs, hills of tailings, lofty
stores of ore, iron sheds, mills, offices, and headgear structures, until finally they occupied an entire
valley. Presently, while we still clung to the ridge,
we saw that the scattered cottages, with their
respective groves, were becoming more massed,
and looking ahead of them we saw the city of
Johannesburg, filling the breadth of a valley,
girdled by a thin line of tall smoke stacks, and
dominated by two parallel lines of hills, the crests
of which rose perhaps 300 ft. or so above the city.
The scent of eucalyptus groves filled the air, for
now the ridge on our right was given up to
cottages, villas, mansions, each separated by firs,
eucalyptus, flower gardens, and varied shrubberies,
the whole making a charming sight, and a worthy
approach to the capital of the mining industry.

POPULATION AND AREA OF JOHANNESBURG.

Reduced to matter-of-fact figures, Johannesburg
proper covers four square miles; its roads and
streets are 126 miles in length, twenty-one miles of
which are macadamised, and ten miles have tram
lines. The city's parks and open spaces occupy
eighty-four acres. There have been twenty miles
of gas-piping laid, while the electric light is
supplied by forty-two miles of wire. The waterworks supply 600,000 gallons of water daily for
domestic use, exclusive of what is required for the

mines and street watering. The population of the
town at the census of July, 1896, consisted of
79,315 males and 22,763 females, of whom 32,357
males and 18,520 females were European, making
a total European population of 50,877. It is
believed that during the seventeen months which
have elapsed this population has been augmented
to about 55,000.

The Streets of Johannesburg.

The streets of the city generally are about 50 ft.
wide, while the principal business streets average
90 ft. in width. Several of these are flanked by
buildings which would be no discredit to any
provincial city in England, while the array of shops
have their windows as artistically dressed with
wares as those of Regent Street in London, which
gave me some idea of the character and good taste
of the people.

Johannesburg as It Was and Is.

A photograph of Johannesburg taken in 1888
revealed a thin collection of galvanised iron structures, widely scattered over a roadless veld, while
that of 1897 shows a mature city, compact, with an
aspect of age, well furnished with churches,
massive buildings, parks with trees over a hundred
feet in height, rich villas and artistic mansions, etc.
It was scarcely credible that in such a short period

BETWEEN THE CHAINS, JOHANNESBURG.

[To face page 80.

such a marvellous change had been wrought. The
wonder was increased when I was driven along the
length of Hospital Hill, and noted the streets of
this suburb, bordered by artistic and costly houses,
luxuriant shrubberies, flower gardens, and stately
lines of shade trees. The marvel was greater still
when my conductor told me that as late as 1892—
five years ago—this suburb, now so flourishing, was
a mere virgin grassy veld. " What, all these miles
of groves and gardens and villas sprung up since
1892 ? " " Yes, so prodigiously rapid is the growth
of vegetation, trees, climbing plants and shrubs,
when daily watered, that these shade trees which
give the suburb such an appearance of age have
only been planted during the last five years ! "

Krupp Guns in Eden.

Now these picturesque and comfortable resi-
dences of such varying architecture, whose furniture
I could just see through open windows and doors,
and bespoke great wealth and taste, you must bear
in mind would adorn Birmingham or Manchester.
Imagine miles of such houses crowded with fair
occupants and troops of daintily-clad children, their
long hair floating in the wind as they sported in
snowy garments on the lawns and amid the flowers,
and then my surprise and something more as I
suddenly came in view of a fort, which the rude
Boers have built to terrorise this community. The

G

superb ridge, which seemed to me with its beautiful
houses and gardens a veritable Paradise after four
thousand miles of travel over treeless plains, and
which would certainly be an ornament to any city
on the globe, had in its centre a large and ugly
earthwork, behind which were monstrous Krupp
guns to lay waste this Eden, should the humanity
of Johannesburg ever be driven by despair to strive
physically for the rights of freemen. The mere
suggestion of it is brutish, and a Government
which can coolly contemplate such a possibility,
and frighten timid women and young children with
such horrid prospects, are only fit to be classed
with the Herods of the Dark Ages.

THEN AND NOW.

A short drive northward of the suburb placed
me in a position to view the far-reaching desolate
wastes of the primitive veld, and to realise more
fully what human intellect, skill, energy, and capital
have done on Hospital Hill and in Johannesburg
itself. Twelve years ago there was not a vestige
of life—human or vegetable, except the grass—to
be seen within the entire range of vision from the
Hill, and yet the creators of the remarkable trans-
formation we had just seen were to be threatened
with slaughter and devastation if once they plucked
up courage to exact the rights which every civilised
Government would long ago have granted to them !

JOHANNESBURG AND ITS GREAT INDUSTRY "SUBJECT TO SENILE MADNESS AND BOORISH INSENSIBILITY."

It were well now, after briefly showing what Johannesburg and its population is, that the chief of the State and his rustic burghers, in whose hands lie the future of this remarkable city and its industry, should be presented to your readers, in order that they might realise the striking incongruity of first-class mechanical ingenuity, spirited enterprise, business sagacity, and tireless industry being subject to senile madness and boorish insensibility. That such a thing should be is most preposterous and contrary to all human precedent. For elsewhere, and since the dawn of civilisation, Intellect has always become Master, Captain and King over Ignorance, but at Johannesburg it is Asinine Ignorance which rules Intellect. Another reversal of human custom is seen in the submissiveness of Intellect to Ignorance, and though, being naturally sensitive under the whip and restless under the goad, it remonstrates sometimes, its remonstrance is in such a sweet mild way that the spectator can only smile and wonder.

"OVERMASTERING SURPRISE" AT THE STATE OF THINGS ON THE RAND.

Fitting words are wanting to describe my overmastering surprise at the state of things in the

Transvaal; I am limited by space and time, so
that I must let my pen race over three pages and
trust largely to the intelligence of those who read
the lines.   I have a printed cutting before me of a
discussion in the First Raad of the Boer Republic,
during which the President, in the support of his
views, stands up and says that Isaiah had been told
by the Lord that Israel had been punished because
the rulers of that people had not hearkened unto
the voice of the poor.   Another speaker of similar
intelligence rose up to contend that the Lord had
enjoined that the rich, not the rulers, should help
the poor, and Isaiah had not been told that the
poor were to be helped with other people's money.
This construction of Scripture raised the President
of the State to his feet again, and he reiterated the
fact that the Lord had meant the rulers, whereupon
another Senator interpolated the remark that some
people were in the habit of shielding themselves
behind the Bible with a view to saving their own
pockets.

NAILING IT WITH SCRIPTURE.

Fancy a discussion of that kind taking place
in the Legislative of a British Colony !   What
vexation and shame we should feel that a Colonial
Government should be based on what Isaiah had
conceived had been told to him respecting Jewish
elders and rulers !   We should undoubtedly feel
that such a discussion was an outrage on common

sense and good taste, and that the Colony had mistaken a parliamentary hall for a synagogue. But at Pretoria such discussions appear to be everyday incidents—the most commonplace arguments are supported by quotations from Isaiah or some other prophet.

KRUGER'S CANT.

At Standerton, the other day, the President was questioned as to the prospects of assistance being given to poor burghers. His entire reply is worth quoting, but I have only room for a small portion of it. Said he : " The burghers' distress has been caused by the war (Jameson's raid), and the subsequent unrest has not tended to improve matters. The burghers have suffered from these circumstances. The country has been compelled to spend a lot of money on the building of forts, nearly £2,000,000, by which our means have been exhausted. In the Zoutpansberg district especially, the condition of things I know to be most distressing. White families as well as black are dying rapidly. Still I expect you to turn to the Bible in a time of adversity like this. Follow the prophet Isaiah's advice, and look to the Lord God who has so far befriended you. Why will men not follow in the path of the Lord instead of losing money at races and by gambling ? " etc., etc.

Two Millions on Forts while People Starve.

One knows not which most to pity, the blundering muddle-headed President, or the wretched feeble-minded people who listen to him. Even little English school-boys would have had the courage and sense to tell the President how unfit to govern anything but a small pastorate on the veld he had proved himself after such a speech, and have pointed out to him that the two million pounds spent on unnecessary forts, had been the means of starving the Zoutpansberg frontier, and that it was blasphemy to make the Lord responsible for his own foolish and stupid extravagance, besides adding insult to injury to accuse people with love of horse-racing and gambling when they were starving through his criminal folly.

The burghers, however, lacking the intelligence of English school-boys, adjourn after the speech to banquet their venerable chief and to glorify him.

At Heidelberg the President was asked if the Secret Service Fund was divided into two sections. "Yes," he replied, "for I have to keep my eyes wide open, and I have private detectives all over the country to prevent any surprise like that of the Jameson raid occurring again."

What an extraordinary man, to devote £80,000 a year fighting an enemy that does not exist, when, according to his own words, his burghers are dying of starvation at Zoutpansberg!

THAT CORNER-STONE.

When questioned as to his objections to the Industrial Report, the President said that "if it had been accepted the independence of the Republic would have been lost." Provided certain obstacles were removed, he was in favour of taking over the railway. The profits of the railway were divided at the rate of five per cent. to the Company, ten per cent. to the shareholders, and eighty-five per cent. to the State. The shareholders, according to him, were not the Netherlands Company. As regards dynamite, it was the corner-stone of the State's independence.

WOLF!

Whenever President Kruger can get an opportunity to utter a word which will reach the public ear, he harps upon the independence of the country being in danger, and the dynamite concession being the corner-stone of that independence. The cry of the wolf being at the door has enabled him to enjoy fifteen years of office, with its princely emoluments, and to the ossified brains of his burghers the same old story may be related with endless repetitions.

THE DYNAMITE DISGRACE.

At one electioneering meeting the President said that he refused to have electric trams at Johannesburg because he could not see his burghers deprived of the means of selling their forage. He also assured his audience that the Dynamite Company should be compelled to manufacture dynamite from the products of the country—although it is well known that almost every constituent of it must be imported from Europe. He also stated that the Dynamite Company was essential to the independence of the State since it made the manufacture of gunpowder possible, whereas he knows well that the ingredients of the composition must be purchased abroad.

At another place the President said : " I get so much money from the mines that in a short time I shall be able to pay for the dynamite factory. I will not break the factory. I will not allow any importation of the ingredients to take place, but at the same time I will not throw up the factory." The people were unable to perceive any nonsense in his words. As the factory can only manufacture 80,000 cases a year, and as 250,000 cases are needed, it never struck them that 170,000 cases would have to be bought elsewhere, nor that as dynamite cannot be made in the Transvaal without obtaining its constituents elsewhere did it seem necessary to ask how the President could keep his promise.

THE PRESIDENTIAL DOTARD WILL BE ELECTED A FOURTH TIME.

If one will read the above carefully over, he will be able to gauge the intellect of this wonderful statesman fairly well, and measure the sense of the people who gape at these absurdities. What with political economy drawn from Isaiah and practical life being ordered by what the prophet Isaiah said, with a future policy based upon the manufacture of dynamite in the Transvaal, and the support of the tariffs of the Netherlands Railway, and the ensuring of a produce market at Johannesburg by not allowing the people of that city to have electric trams, the payment of £225,000 a year to keep the forts in order, and £200,000 interest on the capital expended on the wholly useless structures, the constant denunciation of the murderer Rhodes, the squandering of £80,000 a year to spare the Transvaal from another surprise like the Jameson raid, it appears to the simple burghers that their President is the only fit man for the office he holds, and that Kruger is only second to Washington.

And yet both President and people are within reach and close connection with every possible civilised influence ; but the truth is that their dull, dense, and dark minds are impenetrable to good sense, impervious to reason, and insensitive to the noble examples we see at Johannesburg. Though there may be neither rhyme nor reason in anything the Presidential dotard may say or do, the burgher farmer will cling to him and make him victor over all rivals for a fourth time.

My Advice to "The Bright, Clever Men at Johannesburg."

This is the wonderful incongruity I spoke of that such a President and people as above described should be rulers over the enlightened progressive community of Johannesburg. At a dinner at the Club I quietly suggested a corrective of this incongruous and unprecedented condition of things, and said that it lay in the saying : "It was expedient that one man should die for many." I was conscious of being stared at, and, indeed, if with all their intellectual capacity the idea never entered their minds before, I can quite understand their surprise. But it appears to me that if, according to their own admission, they have tried everything—pleading, arguments, petitions, resolutions, menaces, bribery—and all have failed, relief can only come through one of two things, viz.: Active interference of England, or a determination on their own part to endure no more. As to the first, every public man in England knows that the active interference of England in a matter of this kind is impossible. It may be her moral duty to

interfere, but those bright, clever men at Johannesburg should know as well as we do that the present
age and times will not admit of national action on
grounds purely moral. The story of their wrongs
will always receive sympathy, but to move a
nation to action something more than sympathy
is required. We delivered the Transvaal territory
over to the charge of its own citizens, and they
only are responsible for what happens in their
territory. If their laws are oppressive or unjust to
the strangers residing amongst them, the strangers
may withdraw, or endure the evils of which they
complain as well as they can. It is not for us to
advise them what they should do; the choice
must lie with themselves. They may fly the
country or leave their properties in the charge of
trustworthy Boer agents, if any such can be found,
or they may continue to suffer all that the Boers
may choose to inflict, or they may all unite in
ceasing work and pay neither dues, taxes or bribes
until justice be done to them, but we cannot
interfere until we know what Johannesburg has
resolved upon doing. What we may do in any
event is not worth discussing—no, not until the
Johannesburg people act like Englishmen.

CHAPTER V.

PRETORIA, SOUTH AFRICAN REPUBLIC.
November 23, 1897.

PAUL AND HIS OIL PAINTING.

I WAS fortunate enough to have an early morning
(5.30 A.M.) interview with President Kruger before
he departed on what may probably be his last
electioneering tour.   As he was fully dressed in
the usual black suit and little old-fashioned top
hat, and smoking on the verandah of his house, the
old President must have risen from bed an hour
earlier at least, and though all the clocks in this
region are fully thirty minutes behind time, 5 A.M.
is a remarkably early hour to begin business. Two
armed guards in the uniform of London police
inspectors stood in the street barring the way to
the house ; but a mere look from the President
sufficed to give us admission. His "Good-morning"
in English slipped from him unconsciously, and
after a shake hands he led the way to a spacious
saloon, wherein the first thing that attracted my
attention was a large and coarse oil painting of
him. It happened that the seat shown to me
placed Mr. Kruger and his picture directly in a
line, in front of me, and I was thus forced to

KRUGER'S HOUSE AT PRETORIA.

[*To face page* 92.

compare the original with the copy. The history
of the painting I do not know, but as it is permitted
to be hung so prominently in the reception room,
it is to be presumed that the President and his
friends regard it as a faithful likeness, and are
consequently proud of it. This small fact proved
to be the A B C of my study of the man of destiny
of South Africa. It was clear that neither Kruger
nor his friends knew anything of art, for the picture
was an exaggerated reproduction of every defect
in the President's homely features, the low, narrow,
unintellectual brow, over-small eyes, and heavy,
massive expanse of face beneath. The man himself was almost beautiful in comparison with the
monster on the canvas, and I really could not help
pitying him for his innocent admiration of a thing
that ought to be cast into the fire. But presently
the President spoke—a mouthful of strange guttural
words—in a voice that was like a loud gurgle, and
as the great jaws and checks and mouth heaved
and opened, I stole a glance at the picture, and it
did not seem to me then as if the painter had
libelled the man. At any rate, the explosive
dialect so expanded the cheeks and widened the
mouth that I perceived some resemblance to the
brutal picture.

THE TRANSVAAL "SIR ORACLE."

I was told by my introducer, after the interview
was over, that the President had already read a

chapter in the Bible, and that it is his custom to
do so every morning before appearing in public.
I then understood the meaning and tone of his last
words to me. Said he : "What I have said, shall
be done." He was alluding to the fact that the
Dynamite Monopoly and Railway Rates were the
children of the State, but they should be put into
the hands of the Attorney-General, and if it were
discovered that the terms of the concessions were
in any way contravened, reparation should be
made. The manner of his last words reminded
me of the Jovic way—" and what I will, is fate "—
but when I learned how he had been engaged, I
knew he had been infected with the style of the
Pentateuch.

THE "HUMBUG POSE."

This humour of Mr. Kruger's is becoming more
pronounced as he ages. He has fully arrived at
that stage of life which made Mr. Gladstone so
impossible in the Cabinet. There is abundance
of life and vitality in the President, but he is so
choleric that he is unable to brook any opposition.
Any expression suggesting him to be mistaken
in his views or policy rouses his temper, the
thunderous gurgle is emitted, and the right arm
swings powerfully about, while the eyes become
considerably buried under the upper eyelids. I
suppose, from the photograph of him now on sale
at Pretoria, which represents his eyes looking

upward, he fancies this to be the impressive gaze. He receives a stranger with the air of a pedagogue about to impress his new pupil, and methodically starts to inculcate the principles of true states-manship ; but he soon heats himself with the dissertation, and breaks out into the strong master-ful style which his friends say is such a picturesque feature in his character, and which his critics call the "humbug pose." If by the latter is meant the repetition of stale platitudes, and the reiteration of promises which will never be carried out, I fear I must agree with the critics.

Look on this Picture and ——

Had I been asked to describe Mr. Kruger's character as conceived by me from what I had read of him, I should have summed him up after the style of an old author, thus : " What can be more extraordinary than that a man of no edu-cation, no fortune, no eminent qualities of body, should have had the courage to attempt, and the happiness to succeed, in wresting back this splendid country from the tenacious grasp of one of the greatest powers of the earth ? That he should have the pluck and skill to defeat a British general in the field, even while that general was flattering himself for his successful manœuvre, compel the British Government to relinquish what it had gained, and to reinstate the independence of his

country by a Convention ; and then upon second
thoughts to cancel that Convention and substitute
another which almost made his country a sovereign
State ; then, in flat opposition to the terms of that
Convention, dare to disclose his vindictive hatred of
the British race, among whom he was born and
whom he often served, oppress so many thousands
of his former fellow-subjects, curtail their guaranteed rights, trample upon them as he pleased, and
spurn those who did not please his tastes, make
every diplomatist who ventured to plead for them
ridiculous for his failures ; and while he dealt so
hardly with those whom he characterised as his
enemies, could make his friends understand that he
was master, his burghers awe-stricken by his suc-
cesses, at the same time make both friends and
enemies give ready credence to his professions of
justice and benevolence, to mock three of the most
powerful nations of Europe by turns, and compel
each with equal facility to maintain its distance ;
to make his illiterate and rude burghers feared and
courted by the Governors of the several Colonies
around him, to make their Governors and Legis-
latures humbly thank and congratulate him, to
make one sovereign State solicit a nearer connection with his own, to be the dictator of the colony
wherein he was born, and its Government obse-
quious to his slightest wish, and lastly (for there is
no end to all the particulars of his glory), have
talented and educated men of the world visit him,

and depart for home enchanted with his conde-
scension, enraptured with his humour and piety,
and overflowing with admiration for his greatness
and many excellences of character ; to be able to
have himself elected President for a fourth time,
compel his ministers, generals, and rivals to sing
his praises in their election addresses, and keep his
burghers firm in the belief that he alone is the
saviour of his country, and the only true patriot
whom they can trust—to do all this is, at any rate,
to be extraordinary."

ON THIS.

That was my ideal picture of Stephanus
Johannes Paulus Kruger before the interview ; but
since I have been permitted to see him face to
face, I am lost in amazement at the ridiculous
picture my fancy, fed by cowardly and designing
men, had conjured up.   That so many people
should have united in singing this man's praises
can only be accounted for by the fact that they
must have had some interest, political or pecuniary,
to serve, otherwise how is it that his "greatness"
solely consists in my mind of what he has derived
from the cowardice and weaknesses of others ?
"Many a mickle makes a muckle," and hundreds of
little advantages obtained over petitioners of all
kinds, and by the follies and mistakes of others,
constitute in the mind of the curious multitude

H

what they have been pleased to term "greatness." In appearance he is only a sullen, brutal-looking concierge, dressed in old-fashioned, ill-made black clothes. He appears to know absolutely nothing outside of burgherdom ; he has neither manners nor taste ; his only literature seems to be limited to the Bible, and a few treaties and documents about the Republic ; he has no intrinsic excellence of character that should appeal to the admiration of the public ; but what he does know, he knows well. He knows the simplicity of his rude and bearded brethren of the veld ; he can play upon their fears, and their creed, with perfect effect, and it is in the nature of his ill-conditioned personality to say "no." All the rest has fallen to him because he is so stubborn, so unyielding, and others so vacillating and so pitifully weak.

Kruger's "Strength."

I do not suppose there are any people in the world so well represented by a single prominent man as the Boers of South Africa are represented by Mr. Kruger. He is pre-eminently the Boer of Boers in character, in intellect, and in disposition, and that is one reason why he has such absolute control over his people. His obstinacy—and no man with a face like his could be otherwise than obstinate—his people call strength. Age and its infirmities have intensified it. His reserve—born of self-pride, consciousness of force — limited ambitions, and self-reliance, they call a diplomatic gift. His disposition, morose from birth, breeding, isolation fostered by contact with his kind, is unyielding and selfish, and has been hardened by contempt of the verbose weaklings who have measured themselves against him.

"DENSE, IGNORANT, AND IMPENETRABLE."

This is the man whom the Johannesburgers hope to weary with their prayers and petitions; but they never will do it. Nor will they convince him by their arguments, for he is too dense, ignorant, and impenetrable. This is the man our new High Commissioner hopes to soften with his cultured letters and amiable allusions to the possibilities of restoring concord in South Africa. I feel a reluctance to say it, but his labour will be in vain. This is the man to whom the accomplished and lovable British Agent at Pretoria has been sent with a view to obliterate the memory of Jameson's raid, and smooth the way to a kindly and humane consideration of his countrymen's grievances; but he cannot make any impression on an unimpressible nature like Kruger's.

THE EFFORTS TO EDUCATE KRUGER.

But the singular thing is that despite repeated, nay constant, rebuffs, all who have any dealings with Mr. Kruger persist in hoping that he will relent in the end, and may genially try to exercise his authority for the termination of the existing unpleasantness. I spoke with all sorts and conditions of men at Johannesburg, and I only met one man who expressed his convictions that it was utterly impossible to induce the President to alter, or modify, his views. The rest, so often defeated and humbled, still continue to entertain a lively hope that things will improve. They are mostly clever and highly educated men, but whether it is that they have no time to study the disposition of the man, in whose hand lie their destinies, or their faith in themselves is so great, I know not, but it is certain that no sooner are they baffled in one attempt, than a new project has captivated their fancy, and enlisted their enthusiasm. They have tried to shame Kruger by their ill-considered demonstration in favour of Sir Henry Loch. The National Union has published its solemn declarations of uitlander claims and rights, they have had a Jameson raid, they have had the benefit of Lord Rosmead's diplomacy, they have resorted to giving indiscriminate backsheesh, they have made much of the Progressive party, they have had an Industrial Commission, Chamber of Mines gatherings and speeches, but they are not a whit further advanced, and if to-morrow it is suggested that the mines should be closed, I suppose they would adopt that course or any other with equal belief in its efficacy.

MR. CHAMBERLAIN AND THE PRESIDENT.

Mr. Chamberlain again, despite his better sense, and possibly his inclinations to try different methods, has—judging from the blue books which contain his letters—come round to the belief that the old methods of diplomacy are best, and now conscientiously exchanges courtesies in the blandest and most amiable fashion, as though there were no burning questions unsettled. He professes to cherish a profound belief in the integrity of Mr. Kruger, and assumes an assurance that everything will be done by him according to the spirit of the London Convention. Sir Alfred Milner has been also heard to say that it is all "humbug and nonsense" to express a doubt of good relations being restored, and probably Mr. Greene in the first flush of his coming has written in equally strong terms of the approaching pacification of South Africa. I wish I could share in this buoyant feeling, but the spirit of the Boer, as it has impressed itself on my mind, since I crossed the Vaal, forbids me to believe that while Kruger lives there can be any amelioration in the condition of the Johannesburger. The Boers have endowed Kruger with almost absolute power, and if up to seventy-two years of age Kruger has been the incarnation of hostility to England, it would be a miracle indeed if in his extreme old age he should be converted.

PAUL'S SPOOF.

It strikes me with wonder also that with all our astuteness, our experience, and our knowledge of human nature, we should be so credulous of these many professions of amity from the Transvaal. I am fresh from my visit to Mr. Kruger. It was but yesterday I heard the many dismal complaints of Johannesburg ; I have but now come in from a look at the fortified heights of Pretoria. I open the last blue book and extract the following from the Boer despatches :—

1. " No unfriendliness is intended by Volksraad. It would be unfair to interpret it as such."

2. "This Government also can give the assurances that it has no other than peaceable intentions."

3. "This Government again expresses its opinion that through friendly co-operation, the confidence so rudely shaken, as well as peace and prosperity, will be restored."

4. "The Government readily gives the assurances that there is no intention on its part of infringing its obligations."

5. "This Government need hardly assure Her Majesty's Government that it will comply with its obligations as soon as it is in a position to do so."

6. " His Honour the President requests me to assure you that there is no intention on his part to depart from the terms of the London Conven-

tion, and that he is anxious to act throughout in conformity with those assurances, etc."

"A BOER MACHIAVELLI."

One who knows anything of the conditions under which the Johannesburgers live need not come to Pretoria to know how hollow and insincere these and countless other professions are ; but when read at Pretoria with those four forts constructed at lavish expense commanding the approaches to the capital from the Johannesburg direction, the mendacity of the writer seems appalling. Take these in conjunction with the many promises President Kruger has uttered to interviewers, to casual English visitors, to deputations or in public speeches, in relation to his intentions to adhere strictly to the terms of the Convention of 1884, and one cannot but conclude that, though the President reads the Bible daily, he must have overlooked the sentences that apply to liars. If, despite the cordiality, conciliatoriness, and numerous expres-sions of goodwill, that are visible in Mr. Chamberlain's despatches, and the entreaties, remonstrances, and the continual patient efforts of the uitlanders to soften the asperities of Boer rule, President Kruger and his burghers, while writing in the style of the above quotations, build these great forts at Pretoria and Johannesburg, it is evident that English people have wholly failed to understand this man, and that their ideal of a "goodish sort of man, kindly and a little old-fashioned, a little slow perhaps, and stubborn after the Dutch type," never existed since Pretoria was founded. On the contrary, the real Kruger is a Boer Machiavelli, astute and bigoted, obstinate as a mule, and remarkably opinionated, vain and puffed up with the power conferred on him, vindictive, covetous and always a Boer, which means a narrow-minded and obtuse provincial of the illiterate type.

How the Convention was Contravened.

"Go and tell your people," said he once to a deputation from the uitlanders, "that I will never change my policy."

For once he spoke the truth, and having seen him I feel convinced he never will, but he has persuaded so well and spoken so fairly, that I doubt if a Colonial Office official will abandon hope of him.

I recall to mind the last portion of Article 14 of the London Convention, which refers to those persons other than natives who may enter the South African Republic. "They shall not be subject, in their persons or property, commerce or industry, to any taxes, local or general, other than those which are or may be imposed on citizens of the South African Republic."

How does that agree with a fourpenny tax on

THE CLUB, PRETORIA.

[To face page 104.

a four-pound loaf of bread ?   Or a shilling tax
for every four pounds of meat, or a shilling tax on
every four pounds of potatoes, or a sixpence for
every half-pound of butter eaten at breakfast by
a miner and his family ?

THE RACIAL WAR BOGEY.

People at home do not stoop to consider what
such details mean. They have probably more in
their minds the general effect of a racial war in
South Africa, and see red ruin in place of the peace
and content that ought to prevail here. But what
have we to do with racial war and its horrors ?
Our business is to look at the immediate present,
and not anticipate events which need not take
place. We have to abide by the Convention ; why
should not the other party also abide by it? It
was a fair understanding. Kruger himself drew
up the terms, and they were mutually agreed to,
and it is scarcely common sense to suggest that
the party which seeks to maintain the Convention
instigates a racial war, while the party that has
broken the Convention repeatedly should be held
innocent and blameless.

THE LAWS OF "A CHOLERIC, OBSTINATE OLD MAN."

There is another point in this article which has
attracted my attention here. The first part of
Article 14 says, "All persons other than natives,

conforming themselves to the laws of the South
African Republic, will have full liberty to enter,
travel, or reside in any part of the South African
Republic." I am curious to know what laws were
meant here. Were they any laws which the sacred
twenty-four members of the First Raad might
choose to impose, or were they such laws as might
be made conformable to civilised countries? If
the laws were made by the people of the Transvaal, we, of course, should not hear so much of
grievances, but the existing laws of the South
African Republic have mostly been proposed by
President Kruger, and obsequiously enacted by
the twenty-four members of the First Raad without reference to the people, and consequently
they could not fail to be intolerable to the larger
number. The Grondwet throws a light upon the
character of the laws that were meant when the
fourteenth Article of the Convention was framed.
Its first chapter declares that the Government shall
be Republican, that the territory of the Transvaal
shall be free to all foreigners, and that there shall
be liberty of the Press. Then I think that, as
Her Majesty's Ministers admitted and sanctioned
the terms of the fourteenth Article, they understood the "Laws of the South African Republic"
to mean the Constitution, and such other laws as
obtain in civilised countries, for it is scarcely
credible that they would have signed the Convention had they understood that Englishmen could

not be admitted into the rights of burghership until after fifteen years' residence, or if poverty was to be a barrier to that "full liberty" sanctioned by the Grondwet and the fourteenth Article. We may also rest assured that the British Commissioners would not have signed the Convention if that "full liberty" did not include free speech and a free Press, the full use of one's native language, the full exercise of every faculty according to custom prevailing in all civilised countries, or if certain British individuals who happened to misconduct themselves were liable to receive excessive punishments, or if for writing a market note in English a £5 fine was to be imposed, or if for grumbling an Englishman was to be expelled from the country, or if for considering himself as being a little better than a Kaffir he should be compelled to wear a badge that marked him as inferior to a Boer. I think it may be taken for granted also that no British Commissioner would have attached his name to a Convention had he guessed that the Laws of the Republic might mean any odd or fantastic whim that might enter into the head of a choleric, obstinate old man like the present President for instance.

UITLANDERS' RIGHTS SECURED BY A SOLEMN CONVENTION.

Far from deserving the title of great which some English visitors have bestowed upon Mr. Kruger,

it seems to be that the most fitting title would be
" little." The gifts the gods have given his State
he resolutely refuses. His sole purpose and object
seems to be to make the South African Republic
the China of South Africa. He declines to admit
men who are in every way qualified to the burghership, though every other new country is competing
for such men. The Americans welcomed every
able-bodied incomer as a fresh ally, and valued
each workman as being worth £200 to the State.
Thirty years ago citizenship depended upon
nativity, and could never be abandoned. The
idea was a relic of the Middle Ages, and was
traceable to tribal superstition of prehistoric times,
but as nearly every country in the civilised world
has consented to admit people of all races to
citizenship after a probationary period of from
three to five years, the South African Republic
only marks its own retrogression to barbarism by
extending the term to fifteen years. Mr. Kruger,
instead of granting to foreigners common rights
which were sealed to them by a Solemn Convention, for which let it be always remembered the
independence of the State was assured, prefers to
keep 80,000 uitlanders outside the pale of citizenship, to irritate them by onerous laws passed by an
oligarchy of twenty-four men, and to grind them
with taxes. If he made them burghers his country
would be the premier State in South Africa, and
he might then do almost what he liked, except

invade his neighbours' territories. The worst that could befall a Boer is that some candidate might be thwarted in his hopes of the Presidency, but the inviolability of the Republic and its Independence would be placed beyond danger.

WHAT KRUGER'S POLICY WILL LEAD TO.

Mr. Kruger professes to seek the prosperity and progress of the State, but I will simply mention the dynamite and other monopolies, of which we have heard so much lately, and point out that it is only a Boer audience that could be persuaded to believe in him. The resources of the State are forbidden to be exploited, the Minister of Mines refuses to proclaim new gold fields ; the taxation on those in operation is so heavy that only a few of the richest mines on the main reef can be profitably worked. The expenditure of the State is extravagant—quite 40 per cent. could be saved, I am told. The reforms lately mentioned by the Industrial Commission, if granted, would reduce the cost of working expenses by 4s. per ton, and be the means of re-opening mines which were closed as being unprofitable, as well as bringing several miles of the reef into the payable degree. But Mr. Kruger's idea of increasing the prosperity of the State is by raising the taxes on the mines that continue to pay dividends, in order to compensate the Treasury for the loss of revenue incurred from the collapse of the poorer mines. If, as one mine after another succumbs to the burden of taxation, he increases the taxes on the richer mines, every mine must become closed, because no gold mine was ever discovered that did not cost much money and high-priced labour to extract the gold from it.

THOSE WHO PAY THE PIPER.

Mr. Kruger's ideas of government are to divide the people into two classes—those who get their living from the surface soil and those who get it underground. He himself favours the former. According to him they only are entitled to have any voice in the Government, and to be considered as citizens of the Republic. As for the other class, they have no rights, and the country would be relieved if they departed. Yet, according to the last Budget, I find £3,799,913 of the State's revenue were derived from the class who labour underground, while only £1,086,586 were obtained from the other class.

KRUGER'S CANT.

But if we wish to know and realise Mr. Kruger thoroughly, we should pay attention to his last election address, issued about a week ago. He says : "As I have before told you, I aim, as instructed by the Scriptures, at justice and righteousness to all men—to lay down on our political

territory the eternal principles of God as the
foundation of our State. The taking to heart of
the lessons of that Word enables us to be certain
under all our difficulties. These lead us to a
recognition of our absolute dependence, not on the
great ones and power holders of the world, but
upon Him who sent that Word to us."

"Burghers and fellow-countrymen, the times are
such that a wise and judicious development of our
sources of aid requires the most earnest consideration. Therefore these must be protected and
advanced, and while we lend a helping hand to
the mining industry we must not lose sight of the
agriculture and cattle farming, so that prosperity
and progress may be brought to the doors, not of
some only, but of all. That will be my earnest
endeavour. Many of you have sustained almost
irreparable losses through rinderpest, and you know
what has been done in order to help you to tide
over these hard times. I desire to proceed in this
direction everywhere that such assistance may be
required, to the end that many of the very pith of
the people, at present bowed under the yoke of
adversity and misery, may be helped and heartened
by the strengthening of the feeble knees."

I do not think I need quote any more. As will
be seen by the first paragraph, Mr. Kruger takes
the Scriptures as his guide in matters of policy,
and, as he considers the Boers to be the chosen
people, we may infer what the miserable Canaanites

who dwell along the Raad may expect from the
course adopted by Joshua towards their ancient
prototypes. The second paragraph is more secular,
but the policy of Mr. Kruger is just as distinctly
indicated. The "very pith of the people," the
Boers, must be helped and heartened by the
strengthening of the feeble knees, which means
money must be taken from those who did not
suffer in their flocks and herds, viz., the miners,
and distributed amongst those that sustained
almost "irreparable loss through rinderpest."

MR. CHAMBERLAIN'S LOST OPPORTUNITY.

Mr. Chamberlain has led us to believe that he
has a policy which will set these matters right.
He has great faith in Sir Alfred Milner and
Mr. Greene; he has also faith in himself. In brief,
his policy consists of conciliatoriness and firmness
combined. If I have succeeded in this letter to
properly express my convictions and the grounds
for them, it will not surprise anyone if, with all
my belief in Mr. Chamberlain's genius, I utterly
decline to share this faith. Time was, and that
not many months back, when he might by other
methods, not war, nor necessarily leading to war,
have broken down Kruger's obduracy, and made
him more sensible ; but that time has passed. It is
now too late. Time was, and that not long ago,
when the Johannesburgers might have imposed

CHURCH STREET, PRETORIA.

[*To face page* 112.

terms on Kruger and, unassisted by outsiders, have rectified matters themselves ; but the opportunity was lost through Jameson's interference.

Force no Remedy.

The Press has frequently suggested other means of bringing Mr. Kruger to reason, the author of " Boers and Little Englanders " has stated what he thinks ought to be done, the Johannesburgers themselves are brimful of suggestions, but I think that, though some are partially right, I have not come across any which seems to meet the complex case entirely. We have the sentiments of the Colonies to consider as well as the sentiments of the people of Great Britain, and the whole of Europe in fact. Therefore forcible measures in cold blood are out of the question, because from what I heard I doubt that the people of Johannesburg themselves would be grateful if we resorted to them.

Salvation Lies in a United Johannesburg, Passively Resisting Tyranny.

I quite agree that it is the duty of Her Majesty's Government to strengthen our forces in South Africa to show the Boers that we are serious, and that power is at hand in case of necessity, but as long as our forces remain inactive their effect will wear away, and the Boers will soon fall back again

I

to their sullen and vindictive attitude. What, then, is to be done? Nothing, absolutely nothing, until the Johannesburgers themselves prove to us that they are serious, united, and firm, and make the first move. It will be said, however, that they have no arms. No arms are needed of any kind, but the will to suffer and the courage to endure. Their lives will be safe in any case, for even Boers do not shoot unarmed and unresisting men, but if they all say that the taxes are ruinous, that their property is confiscated by these legal exactions— why pay the taxes, why continue to pay bribes to those in authority for trifling relaxations, why assist in any way to perpetuate the "corrupt and rotten" Government of which they complain so bitterly? It amounts to this. The Boers have a right to administer their country as they think best, but if their administration is unjust and oppressive, surely the oppressed have the right of passive resistance, for it is in human nature to resist injustice. The consequence of passive resistance will be imprisonment. But when a sparsely populated State is obliged to imprison some score of thousands of non-taxpayers, and to feed them, bankruptcy is not far off. If any die in prison from starvation, or blood is shed, or general confiscation of property takes place, we then shall have a legitimate cause for action. I do not say that this policy of waiting upon Johannesburg is a noble one, but as we have been so indifferent to the obligations of the Convention, as we have closed every sense to our countrymen's complaints, as we have been the slaves of every petty circumstance, as South Africa is so contentious and fault-finding, as the English uitlanders themselves have threatened to lift their rifles against us if we move to exert pressure on the Boers, it seems to me that we must wait upon Johannesburg and let the people of that city point the way. Every civilised people in Europe can furnish instances of how to resent injustice and defeat oppression. England, Ireland, Wales, France, Spain, Italy, Germany, etc., all have their examples of what courage can do when nerved by despair, and I think, if it is really serious, it is the turn of Johannesburg to show what it can do ; otherwise we must wait until Mr. Kruger's nature changes, which will be " Never, no, never."

CHAPTER VI.

Summary of a Few Impressions.

ON my return from South Africa I was interviewed by a representative of *South Africa*. I had proposed to write on my voyage to England a closing communication describing my visit to Natal and summarising my views on the South African outlook generally. Unfortunately, I was attacked with severe rheumatic pains shortly after the steamer left Cape Town, and was not able to put pen to paper. I, however, gave the representative of *South Africa* the impressions I should have written on the voyage, had circumstances permitted me to do so.

THE LABOUR QUESTION IN NATAL.

" How were you impressed with Natal ? "

" I was very much struck by its beauty and its fitness for a white population. There was one curious anomaly, however, in the fact that the natives in Natal are very numerous, and yet the

Colonists suffer from a deficiency of labour. Ships often lie at the wharves for days, waiting for coal, because labourers cannot be got to put it on board. At the same time the labour party, or the white man's party, at Durban are complaining that the coolies are being brought to Natal in too great numbers."

" Those are points in economic development that want immediate tackling ? "

" Something should be done to start the enlistment of Zulus of Natal in its labour forces for the development of the State. It is a most interesting little State, very quietly governed, and the people are an exceptional class of Colonists, but they seem to have some problems before them which will tax the ability of future Ministries."

" The coolie immigration question, I take it, is not one of the least of these ? "

" That is so. There are masses of white men in England and on the Continent, it seems to me, who would jump at the opportunity of getting allotments of land in Natal. The Government might do worse than afford some greater facilities for the importation of white labour. In Natal there are 45,000 white men against 400,000 Zulus. In addition to that they have taken Zululand with about half a million of Zulus, so that there are now 45,000 whites against 900,000 blacks."

" Then, in your opinion, that mass of blacks wants leavening by the introduction of white men.

The immigration would have to be worked from this end, would it not ? "

"Yes, they would have to be liberally treated for the first few years to induce them to go. Natal, as I have said, is a very lovely country. There are enormous estates railed off for sheep and cattle raising, and it seemed to me that I saw more places there fit for small estates of white men than in any other part of the country, excepting Rhodesia."

Mr. Stanley was careful to further emphasise the exception to his rule furnished by Rhodesia.

"That opens up a very interesting question," remarked the interviewer, "for emigration from this country has been allowed to take its own course without much assistance, save from the emigration agencies, who, of course, have to be approached by intending emigrants instead of approaching them."

Natal Should be Better Advertised.

"Yes," rejoined Mr. Stanley ; "the wants of a Colony like Natal must be advertised, and its claims to the consideration of those desiring new homes should be pressed upon the people of England."

"How do you think the white men in Natal now would regard the influx ? "

"Well, they must be considered, but it is as much for their interests as for those of anyone else. If they are as narrow-minded as the labour party at Durban, there may probably be a serious calamity some day."

"Had you an opportunity of discussing such problems with Mr. Escombe or any of the leading politicians of the Colony?"

"I saw perhaps twenty, but I fancy they are rather afraid of saying what is in their minds, because the ultimate solution depends upon the democracy of Natal, and Ministers hesitate to be leaders in any such agitation."

Although he has already treated the subject of Rhodesia and its future prospects so exhaustively, Mr. Stanley had nevertheless still many points of importance to touch upon. He insisted very strongly upon the necessity for offering inducements to other settlers besides those engaged in mining.

MORE SETTLERS WANTED IN SOUTH AFRICA.

"I think," said he, "every Colony in South Africa has been very remiss in the matter of attracting immigrants. You have only to look at the statistics of population—black and white—to see how disproportionate are the two races. The Cape of Good Hope, with 221,000 square miles, has nearly a million and a quarter of coloured people to 377,000 whites, and the former are multiplying with extraordinary rapidity. Natal, again, as I have said, has 45,000 whites and nearly a million coloured people. British Bechuanaland, with only a little over 5000 whites, has 65,000 coloured people. Matabeleland, or rather what is now Rhodesia, had some years ago only 2500 whites and 250,000 natives. Of course, the whites are more numerous now, but still the disparity is sufficiently striking."

" It has been asserted very freely that until the production of gold assumes large proportions the white population cannot increase, because they have nothing to subsist upon."

" There is always a place for intending farmers. If the land is to be parcelled out among such, the present is as good a time for them as it is for the miners."

" Men, of course, can support themselves on farms, even although there is no town in the vicinity to furnish a market for their surplus produce ? "

" Exactly so. It is necessary in the end to have markets, of course ; but the first necessary thing is to make a home. Considering the conditions of this country and the rapid growth of population, with the closure of the United States, with only Canada and Australia open to the surplus population, where is there a better country for Englishmen than Rhodesia ? "

IMMIGRATION WANTED TO COUNTERBALANCE
BOER INFLUENCE.

"You think Mr. Rhodes has perhaps overlooked the advantage of putting forward these
considerations ?"

"Not only Mr. Rhodes, but all the politicians of
the Cape Colony and Natal. The best work the
British Government ever did was in sending those
five thousand English people to South-East Africa
in the early part of this century. The experiment
unfortunately has never been repeated. There is a
different kind of population going out now. When
they go to the Cape, they begin to spread themselves over every part of South Africa as far as
Salisbury. It seems to me that there ought to be
three or four hundred families going out every
week to settle in new homes. There is a great
political question in the background, and if
Englishmen are not awake to it they must be
instructed. The Boers, not alluding to any political
party such as the Afrikander Bond, or the
Krugerites, or the Republicans of the Orange
Free State and the Transvaal, but judging by their
general conduct and the tone of their public
utterances, seem to have determined to keep
Englishmen out of South Africa in order to maintain the balance of power in their own favour.
Their whole action tends to that. Supposing the

Cape Colony had a grievance against the British Empire, and chose to form a Republic of its own, it would be a Boer Republic, because the Boers are more numerous than the English. It would be an addition to the Orange Free State and the Transvaal. Some great absorbing question might arise at any time ; yet no one seems to have done anything to prepare for such a contingency, or to maintain the balance of power in favour of the English. The Dutch would naturally take sides with one another, as they did in the Jameson raid affair. Then all the Dutch population veered round in favour of the Transvaal, whereas before that, as in the Drifts question, the Cape Dutch rather thought that the Transvaal was wrong. The unjustifiable attack upon the Transvaal, so unexpected, like a bolt from the blue, gave the Dutch an impression that the British Government were at the back of the raiders, or if not the British Government, at least the British nation. They said to themselves, 'the British people are ever hostile to us, and are determined to have this country English, and under the thumb of the British Government. We refuse to have the British Government vex us now as it has done in the past. They drove the Transvaal Dutch from the Cape Colony ; and they may drive us away if we are not united in opposing this constant British hostility or meddlesomeness with our peculiar habits, principles, and ideas.' "

" It is perhaps more correct to say that the
Dutch retired before the advance of the English
rather than that the English drove them away by
persecution."

A HINT TO DOWNING STREET.

" An over-sensitive English sentiment is at the
root of many of the past disturbances.   When I
was going to South Africa on the *Norman* the
great question of the hour was the indenturing of
the Bechuanaland rebels.   I talked a good deal
with Colonial people on board, and they were not
disposed to be reticent about their feelings.   They
frankly said the British people were just beginning
the same old game of meddlesomeness.   ' Here,'
they said, ' are rebels whom we have caught in the
act of fighting against us, raiding and murdering
our fellow-colonists.   We pay for the forces to
suppress that rebellion ; we have taken hold of the
prisoners who have surrendered.   We do not know
what to do with them better than to distribute
them, with their own consent, among the farmers
for a term of five years, instead of imprisoning
them, and thereby making them non-productive
and a burden to the State.   If we had sent them
back to their own country, they would simply have
died, or made it very dangerous for anyone with
property to go near their country, and we should
have had to begin again.   You English say it is a

form of slavery. We deny it. It is no more than Sir Charles Warren did in 1878. What the British Government did in 1878 we are doing now. Don't you suppose that, having given us an almost independent Government, we have got plenty of pious, well-educated, intelligent men as capable of looking after our morals as the civilised people of England? Why do you all the time place English sentiment in opposition to us, with a view of tyrannising over us? We make our laws, and can correct them if they are wrong. We do not want you to interfere all the time. Our lives and our property, the welfare of our wives and children, depend upon good government. But immediately we do anything you raise the cry that we are barbarous and wicked, and are reducing rebels to the state of slaves, and thus you excite and disturb the people.' 'Supposing,' said one of the speakers, 'that the majority of the British nation were inclined to that opinion, and believed that we were so wickedly disposed as to subject our coloured people to a condition of slavery, Parliament would raise the question, and very possibly, if the sentiment has taken deep hold of your people, would pass a law to prevent it. Then a collision of interests would take place—Boers against English. The English would probably follow the British Government, except a few who have been resident in South Africa and understand those questions as well as the born Colonists.

Thus the Colonists would become divided. The Boers and Afrikanders could not trek again, as Bechuanaland and Rhodesia shut them off from the north. They therefore would demand a republic, to cut themselves adrift from the Imperial Government. The same question would be raised as was raised in the United States when they separated from Great Britain. Danger only can arise from the English habit of interfering in Colonial matters which they do not understand, and from not giving the Colonists credit for being able to manage their own affairs.' "

"Then, in your opinion, the remedy for that is to reinforce the English population in South Africa, and for Exeter Hall here to exercise more reserve?"

"Precisely," replied Mr. Stanley. "If you have a manager of an estate and you suppose he is a man of ability and you entrust him with the management of your estate, and then cavil at everything he does, he will resign. That is just the sort of feeling that is so apt to be raised in South Africa — the incompatibility of temper between the people of South Africa and the too sentimental people of Great Britain. There are two parties in South Africa, Boer and British, and if the former are inclined to be tyrannical to the natives and subject them to slavery, you have the English party, which is as clever and intelligent as people here, ready to preach to and convert the oppressors and to act in opposition to them. Therefore, the English criticism at home is not needed, and it should not interfere with the Colonists' domestic concerns. England must give the Colonists credit for their intelligence, and for a desire to act like civilised people. There would be no need then for a Republican, or a Separatist party at the Cape."

A Great Emigration Company Wanted.

"What do you propose as a means towards the end you speak of?"

"It is natural," replied Mr. Stanley, "that the English of Cape Colony should be anxious for the future of the country in case of a separation from Great Britain, and that they should fear the establishment of a Boer Republic. I see in this a very strong reason why someone with power, wealth and influence should step forward and try to lead them to do something to prepare for maintaining the balance of power. Rhodesia, the Transvaal, the Orange Free State and Natal draw away from the Cape Colony a large number of enterprising Englishmen, and consequently the Boers, not being so enterprising, nor so very fond of running from one home to another unless a great political principal is at stake, prefer to stay on their farms and multiply there, whereas the English are all the time thinned down by those everlasting discoveries and developments in the north and north-east, so that they remain numerically inferior to the Dutch. If there was a Company with a man like Mr. Rhodes at the head of it, which would buy land and settle on it new colonists of English birth, they would be all the time keeping up the equality that is necessary to prevent the English from being Boer-ridden."

"Do you think Rhodesia would adapt itself to such a policy as well as the Cape Colony."

"Quite as well. With the opening of all those mines reported to be so promising, and with the vast advertisement of the opening of the railway, Mr. Rhodes ought to see that more miners have been coming into the country than agriculturalists, and something ought to be done to provide for the provisioning of so many people and keeping the prices of food down by multiplying the producers of food. The country is just as well adapted for them as any other in South Africa. If the Government of Rhodesia neglect this, the Boers will go on filtering through the Transvaal to Rhodesia, and the same mistakes will recur that have been made in the Cape Colony and the Transvaal, where the settled population is Dutch and the moving English."

AUSTRALIANS AVAILABLE.

"What are the principal countries outside South Africa from which such settlers could be drawn?"

"There are plenty of people in Australia, for

instance, who would be very glad of the opportunity to settle in nice places in Rhodesia if they were tempted to do so. You must show that Rhodesia is better than Australia, where you have the fringes of the coast and the best parts of the interior already taken up. You have only to go to Melbourne, Sydney, and other large Australian towns, to find that they have a very large population who do not know what to do with themselves or where to go, who would be valuable to a new country like Rhodesia. Take, for example, the people who went from Australia to Paraguay. These would be far better in Rhodesia amongst Englishmen than in Paraguay surrounded by Spanish Americans, whose ideas and modes of life are so entirely different. When I was in Melbourne I had an offer from fifteen hundred Australians to settle in East Africa. I advised them not to do so until the railway was built. They wanted to start ranches and raise cattle there, but I said their stock would die before they could reach the pastures. In Rhodesia to-day, however, you have a country to which such people would be very advantageous. Cape Colony has an enormous area that requires to be populated, and so has Natal. How are you to reach the class of people required for this? What are you to offer them? It must be something better than where they are now."

"In your opinion Rhodesia is well adapted for cattle raising?"

MR. RHODES'S HOUSE, GROOTE SCHUUR, RONDEBOSCH.

[To face page 128.

"Yes ; the Matabele found it so, and there are still many cattle there despite the rinderpest. New cattle will do well enough, I think, if you take them rapidly by railway across the malarial belt."

"And seeing that the Cape is so much nearer to England than Australia, there is no reason why an export trade should not be developed in time?"

CHARMING EAST LONDON.

"Certainly not," was Mr. Stanley's emphatic rejoinder. Proceeding to deal more particularly with the future possibilities of various parts of the Cape Colony, he alluded to his visit to East London, which he thought one of the healthiest places he had ever seen, characterising the country around as a most charming one. "I was more taken with the south-east coast," said he, "than with any other part of South Africa. Probably it was due to the season, but everything was as green as in England. People looked healthy, and little children as rosy as they could be. I admired the magnificent groves of trees planted by colonists and the flourishing estates that were visible all the way until we got into the Karroo. The best part of the eastern province is perhaps as large as Scotland. I should say it was just as well adapted for white people as any part of England, and yet the population is so scant as compared with the vast acreage. It was in that part that the English families were

K

settled, and made beautiful towns like Grahamstown
and Kingwilliamstown."

" And at that time," interpolated the interviewer,
" they had to contend with natives, who are now
subdued ? "

" Yes," said Mr. Stanley, " that is a disadvantage
that settlers nowadays would be exempted from."

" Is there not an obstacle to your scheme in the
circumstance that people nowadays are not content
to go abroad for a mere living ? They demand
something more than they can get at home—not
perhaps a fortune, but at least the chances of
amassing sufficient money to raise them to a
position of comparative independence ? "

How Farmers Make Profits.

" But there are different ways of making a
fortune or of saving money," replied Mr. Stanley.
" It can be done by agriculture as well as by
mining. The farmer, however, must be content to
look upon the farm as his home, and the capital
and labour devoted to it as constantly increasing in
value. The farm which he buys at 10s. an acre
may become worth in a few years from £5 to £10
an acre. There is his profit. He buys an estate
say of 200 acres for £100, and in five or ten years'
time it may be worth £500 or £1,000. It depends
upon the progress made in the general development of a country by the working of its mineral

resources and by its commerce and trade. The greater the development of the country the greater will be the value of the farmer's land, because more people are constantly coming who don't care to be pioneers, but will buy a farm already developed. The pioneer then goes from farm to farm, and in this he makes his profit. People who went from New England to Ohio or Kentucky, for instance, developed farms which they sold at an enhanced price, afterwards removing to Kansas ; after getting, perhaps, twenty-five times as much for their farms in Kansas as they had paid for them, they went next to Colorado, where their farms ultimately fetched twenty-five or fifty times as much as their original cost. Then they went on to Salt Lake, Mexico, Arizona, or other parts of America, and repeated the same process. That is the way a farmer makes his money in such countries."

Mr. Stanley has already dealt at great length with the question of irrigation, which is so important in countries where the water supply is inconstant. In the course of his remarks with our representative he further elaborated this point, showing how the backwardness of agriculture in certain parts of South Africa, as well as in other comparatively new countries, is the fault of the people rather than of the countries.

" The other week," said he, " I suggested the formation of a united South African waterworks

company.   There are hundreds of streams in
Rhodesia and other parts of South Africa, and yet
every casual tourist says the land is worth nothing
for agriculture.   That is what was said about
Mildura, in Australia, until irrigation was started.
The same system is necessary in South Africa, and
a powerful irrigation company could distribute the
water when available, and also conserve it for the
dry seasons."

"I daresay it is your opinion that little can be
done in this direction by the isolated efforts of
individuals ? "

"Practically nothing," replied Mr. Stanley.   "If
new settlers see land near water they will buy it ;
but they come to the country with slender capital,
perhaps two or three hundred pounds, and cannot
afford to sink wells in the desert ; but if someone
will raise that water for them, and sell the land,
it will be taken at once.   The people who settle,
supposing they are English, will constantly keep
English influence equal to the Boer."

RHODESIA IN THE HANDS OF LAND GRABBERS.

"Some existing African Companies hold farm
lands," remarked the interviewer.   "Ought they
turn their attention promptly to the agricultural
development of those lands, instead of confining
their attention so exclusively to mineral wealth ? "

"Certainly," said Mr. Stanley. "Take, for instance, the Willoughby Consolidated. They have an enormous acreage of land. The people of Bulawayo wanted water, so a certain number formed a company to make the waterworks. They had to buy about 6000 acres from the Willoughby Consolidated to protect their watershed. Supposing these people had not bought the land for the sake of the waterworks, the Willoughby Consolidated would have kept all this vast acreage to themselves, and would have developed it only according to the necessities of the neighbourhood, or sold it to some settlers who wanted to live there. Most of Rhodesia has been divided in that way by the people who grabbed at the territory, so that poor settlers, the bone, marrow, and sinew, are frightened by the prices."

"Do you, then, think that the best farms are already allotted?"

"One who was only in the country such a short time as myself cannot go into all these small details. He can only say that his impression is that the people complained that most of the best lands had been taken up by the great companies. Miners are disposed to hold very cheering ideas in regard to the minerals, and more miners come in than agriculturists. Therefore it strikes me, seeing those miners come in in such numbers, that something has been left undone ; the responsible authorities ought to have seen that the proper

settlers who could feed those people were induced
to come at the same time. Earl Grey or some
other Director should be asked if the Chartered
Company had kept habitable land in Rhodesia
which might be sold for farms; if they had
reserved sufficient farming acreage for the wants
of a farming population, or if they had sold it all
to the great companies. It would be people like
Earl Grey who could give you these details. We
can only get impressions from the mutterings of
those in the country who say, ' What is the use of
coming here? all the good land is gobbled up by
the companies.' One would be glad to have the
matter explained. Farmers with £500 capital, if
they could get land cheap in Rhodesia, might be
tempted to settle there, but if the land is in the
hands of companies, those companies will want to
make big profits. The Chartered Company are
under the necessity of selling land to get money.
The greater the run of farmers to Rhodesia the
higher would be the prices of land. The Chartered
Company, we can see, have been liberal enough to
miners, but I doubt whether they have been so
liberal to the farmer class."

"From your experience of the conditions in
England, do you think people at home would
respond readily to an effort by Mr. Rhodes and
the Rhodesian Government to attract them to
Rhodesia ? "

"Yes, I do, because South Africa is as pleasant

a place to live in as any part of the world that I
have visited. It is certainly more pleasant than
the cold north of Canada. America was very good,
but it is not superior to South Africa. The United
States Government, however, had a very large
reserve of land which they could afford to give at
2½ dollars an acre, and they gave 160 acres of land
to anyone who would promise to settle there for
five years and build houses and improve the land.
That is what the Chartered Company should do.
If you have an estate, you must invest a portion of
your capital in seed and in machines for cultivating
the land ; if you regard a State as a farm, the best
seed you can put into it is a farming population.
Settlers who develop the soil contribute as much
wealth to the State as those who dig for minerals.
Perfected communication also adds value to every
acre. I had at one time to explain why I did not
consider the land of the Congo State worth a two-
shilling piece, because it was impossible to reach it,
but, I said, if you make it accessible to me it is
worth so much an acre. If you leave me isolated
in the heart of the Congo, I throw away my life
and the two-shilling piece."

"Is there in Rhodesia plenty of land beyond
what is required for the Matabele and the
Mashonas ? "

What the Chartered Company should do.

"Well," replied Mr. Stanley, "the natives have always got the slopes of the country. It is, of course, a white man's land, because the white man has taken it. At the same time there are reserves, and the question is, how much of the reserves for the whites has been put aside for agriculturists. Ought the Company to be satisfied with having only miners in Rhodesia who will employ the natives, and after all the gold is got will retire and leave Rhodesia the black man's country that it was, or do the authorities intend to plant an English race permanently there? What are their offers? The Chartered Company ought to give 160 acres of land to any settlers who will undertake to develop it and remain on it for five years, after which the land would be their own. A somewhat similar system is adopted with regard to the mines. If you peg out claims you must work them. So it ought to be with the agricultural land. Having done this, it would remain for the Chartered Company to do their utmost to increase facilities for communication. If they gave reserves free to the natives whom they had conquered, they certainly ought to give at least the same] advantages to the white settlers who are to make the country prosperous and to yield revenue by the payment of taxes."

RHODESIAN RAILWAYS.

"Did you observe the criticisms of the *Financial News* on your proposal regarding the railway from Bulawayo to the sea?" asked the interviewer.

"Yes," said Mr. Stanley. "The *Financial News* does not see the object of making two railways between Bulawayo and the coast, but I was writing from the Bulawayo standpoint. If Bulawayo is to be the capital of Matabeleland, it has as much right to branch out in all directions as Salisbury has in Mashonaland. Naturally, if I were a Bulawayan, I should not care to see Salisbury getting all the plums, especially as Bulawayo is better situated than Salisbury. A railway from Bulawayo to Victoria would bring out the merits of the latter place. There are already over a thousand whites between Bulawayo and Victoria, and a great many gold claims. Then, again, it is only twelve miles from Victoria to Zimbabwe. A great many people want to see the ruins. Tourists go to Victoria first, and thence drive in carriages to Zimbabwe. Thus, from all these sources, mines, settlers, merchants, and tourists, the railway would have a good revenue, while the company would have other indirect gains. From Victoria to Umtali you could make a junction with the existing line to Beira. Bulawayo should shoot out its right arm towards the Indian Ocean, for another reason. Supposing, in the event of an outbreak, a scheme were formed by the

L

Boers to cross over the border and occupy the Bechuanaland Railway, where would Rhodesia be? Rhodesia would be cut off, unless it was abandoned, which is improbable. You thus see the necessity of two entrances, one from the east and one from the south. Supposing Bulawayo, on account of its two exits, begins to thrive, and the development of the land is increasing at a great pace, the next thing necessary is to extend its tentacles in other directions, and get more trade. It will not omit the Zambesi Coal Fields and the Victoria Falls. There is another object you have, not only for the tourist to see the Falls, but also the coal fields lying close to them. You reach the Victoria Falls and you have Loanda and the Trans-African Railway, which already reaches 160 miles to the interior; you can either join with that or you can construct a separate line to Mossamedes. You thus draw another line of country to increase the trade of Bulawayo. I am speaking now from the point of view of Bulawayo as a centre of trade. The competition between it and Salisbury might be compared to that which existed for a quarter of a century between St. Louis and Chicago. The former was a very conservative city; it had its enormous fleet of steamers and the whole Mississippi tributary to it, and when it had 250,000 of a population, Chicago had only 50,000. The people of Chicago, however, were determined to tap every field of trade within reach. They

struck off to California, Denver, Utah, St. Louis,
to the north-west, and down to New Orleans, so that
to-day Chicago has a population of one and a half
millions, and St. Louis only 500,000. Bulawayo is
more favourably situated for railway expansion
than Salisbury, which is inclined too far to the
north-east, whilst Bulawayo is almost as near to
Beira as Salisbury is. It is, moreover, as near to
Mossamedes as to the Cape, and it has the whole
Congo State to the direct north of it. Consequently
it would become a kind of Chicago, drawing the
trade of all those countries, so that as the new
white men scattered, some to the Zambesi, raising
a town near the coal fields, and hotels near the
Falls and Zimbabwe ruins, Bulawayo would feed
them all. At the same time, Cape Town would
become the New York of South Africa. If this
were accomplished, then, in any eventuality, Bulawayo and Rhodesia would be secure in their
independence, for they would have their two exits
to the Indian Ocean and to the Atlantic, and could
still remain British."

"Probably Cape Town would look askance at
any proposal to establish a port at Mossamedes?"
said the interviewer.

"Yes," replied Mr. Stanley, "but Rhodesia does
not belong to the Cape, and what is good for its
prosperity must be considered apart from Cape
Town, and, as Rhodesia thrives so long as it is
connected with the Cape, the latter will always

profit by it. Tourists will prefer to go to Cape
Town because there they will be among English-
men instead of Portuguese, but goods would go to
Mossamedes and thus cut off five days in transit."

BLACK AND WHITE.

"Do you think the black men in South Africa
are likely to disappear as the whites increase?"

"No," replied Mr. Stanley, "I do not think they
will. There are now so many wedges of white
population between the native territories that any
native movement can at once be checked. I see
abundance of hope in that direction for the prevention of any federation of the natives such as
used to be tried in the early days of the American
Colonies. There the cause was want of communication, with an enormous area covered by Indians
and only a few scattered settlements of whites, but
in South Africa you have nothing of that kind.
The natives will all be wanted. There are certain
things that they alone can do, such as working in
the open air in the summer. The white men are
the makers of money, and the natives must
naturally be the hewers of wood and drawers of
water."

LONDON: PRINTED BY WILLIAM CLOWES AND SONS, LIMITED,
STAMFORD STREET AND CHARING CROSS.

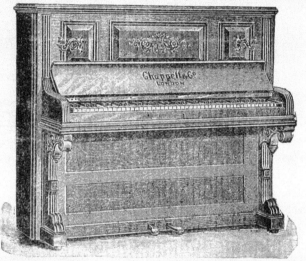

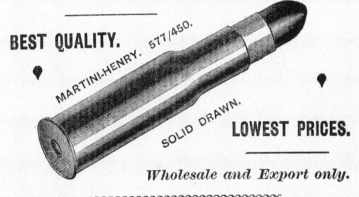

For EU product safety concerns, contact us at Calle de José Abascal, 56–1°,
28003 Madrid, Spain or eugpsr@cambridge.org.

www.ingramcontent.com/pod-product-compliance
Ingram Content Group UK Ltd.
Pitfield, Milton Keynes, MK11 3LW, UK
UKHW012345130625
459647UK00009B/557